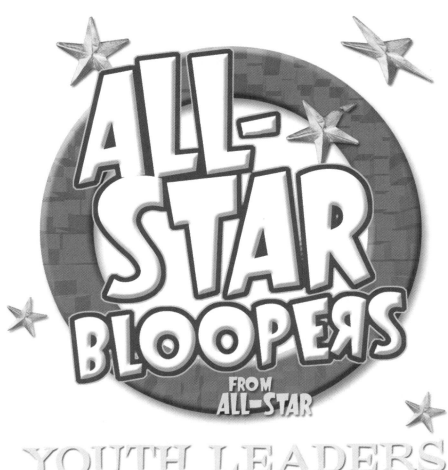

ALL-STAR BLOOPERS

FROM
ALL-STAR

YOUTH LEADERS

Group
Loveland, Colorado

Group's R.E.A.L. Guarantee to you:

Every Group resource incorporates our R.E.A.L. approach to ministry—a unique philosophy that results in long-term retention and life transformation. It's ministry that's:

This is EARL.
He's R.E.A.L.
mixed up.
(Get it?)

Relational
Because student-to-student interaction enhances learning and builds Christian friendships.

Experiential
Because what students experience sticks with them up to 9 times longer than what they simply hear or read.

Applicable
Because the aim of Christian education is to be both hearers and doers of the Word.

Learner-based
Because students learn more and retain it longer when the process is designed according to how they learn best.

ALL-STAR BLOOPERS FROM ALL-STAR YOUTH LEADERS

Credits
Compiling Author: Mikal Keefer
Editor: Kelli B. Trujillo
Creative Development Editor: Jim Kochenburger
Chief Creative Officer: Joani Schultz
Copy Editor: Alison Imbriaco
Art Director: Kari K. Monson
Cover Art Director: Jeff A. Storm
Computer Graphic Artist: Stephen Beer
Illustrator: Alyssa Mooney
Production Manager: Dodie Tipton

Unless otherwise noted, Scripture taken from the HOLY BIBLE, NEW INTERNATIONAL VERSION®. Copyright © 1973, 1978, 1984 by International Bible Society. Used by permission of Zondervan Publishing House. All rights reserved.

Library of Congress Cataloging-in-Publication Data

All-star bloopers from all-star youth leaders.
    p. cm.
  ISBN 0-7644-2302-9 (alk. paper)
    1. Church group work with youth. 2. Church group work with youth--Humor. I. Group Publishing.

  BV4447 .A443 2001
  259'.23--dc21

                                                                                2001023612

10 9 8 7 6 5 4 3 2 1   09 08 07 06 05 04 03 02 01

Printed in the United States of America.

146656

TABLE OF CONTENTS

K243

11/18/24 Joey Gowan - Gift

INTRODUCTION

BLOOPER: *n*. [A blunder] *–syn*. mistake, error, false step, faux pas, oversight, miscalculation, failure, temporary lapse in judgement, glitch, howler, bonehead move, bungle, botch, fatal flaw. Especially prone to happen in public.

Bloopers.

Even the best of us make—and survive—them.

And, in a role as public and demanding as youth work, that's a relief.

Take comfort: No one gets launched in youth ministry without making a few mistakes. That includes the youth ministry gurus who contributed their blooper stories to this collection. Their first years in ministry were just like yours: exciting, confusing, and packed with blooper potential.

They survived—and so will you. You may be humbler for the experience, but you'll find that God uses even your failures for his glory.

A word of advice: Take notes as you read. Many of the potholes that nearly swallowed these youth ministry veterans are still out there. Learn from the experiences of those who went before you: it will save you a considerable amount of pain.

We serve a perfect God who uses very imperfect people.

Welcome to the club. You're in good company.

1. GARDEN GROVE GRAFFITI

Les Christie

One of Les Christie's first youth groups did service projects for the city of Garden Grove, California. "We picked up trash and distributed food to needy families—both without any mishap. The city was pleased, and we were proud. We were ready for more," he remembers.

Between the church building and the local high school was the Garden Grove Freeway. Beneath the freeway was a pedestrian tunnel. The tunnel, which was a student thoroughfare, was full of graffiti and drawings.

Les proposed that his youth group repaint the tunnel.

"The mayor was delighted to accept. The city had to paint the tunnel twice a year, and they had us test a new game plan. We were given 130 large cans of spray paint and told to spray vertical lines up and down the length of the tunnel. That way, even if someone wrote graffiti on the walls later, the stripes would make the graffiti difficult to see."

Twenty-three youth group volunteers showed up at the tunnel Sunday afternoon. Les got them started and then left them with four adult sponsors.

The phone rang early Monday morning. The mayor wanted Les

to meet him at the tunnel—that morning.

"From the tone of his voice, I suspected he wasn't planning to present me with a service award," says Les.

He saw the problem. The kids had painted the stripes as asked. Then they'd graced the walls with their *own* graffiti. Everywhere he looked, Les saw such sentiments as, "Jesus is the answer," and "God loves you."

"One kid had written the entire chapter of Acts 3 on the floor. The city officials somehow failed to appreciate the creativity," says Les.

It took a three-man crew two full days to sandblast the tunnel bare.

Les says, "I needed to train my adult volunteers better instead of turning the project over to them and hoping it would all turn out. I thought they'd have enough common sense to not let the kids do that."

Sometimes it's not what we *say*—it's what we forget to say—that gets us in trouble.

Ready for an education? Find three adults who see your ministry clearly, and ask them how well you delegate. Do you give complete information? authority to act? clear instructions?

List the three adults you'll ask here:

_____

_____

2.JACKPOT
Tim Smith

In 1977, during his youth ministry internship at a Baptist church, Tim Smith joined forces with another youth pastor to plan a junior high "travel camp."

"We did a good job of planning," remembers Tim. "We spent three or four days traveling the route and six months doing publicity and working out logistics." Nearly fifty kids signed up, and the trip ticked along like clockwork—until they reached Las Vegas.

"We took the kids to a casino," says Tim. "The security guy made the minors stay on the linoleum; only people old enough to gamble could walk on the carpet to the gaming tables. The only things the kids could see clearly were the slot machines."

Tim traded three dollar bills for silver dollars, then he lined the kids up so they could see him standing next to a dollar slot machine.

"I held up the three silver dollars and said, 'It can be hard to earn three dollars. Think of what you could *buy* with three dollars. Now take a look at how quickly you can *lose* three dollars.' "

Tim had a volunteer slip the first silver dollar into the one-armed bandit. Thinking that seeing the three dollars disappear so quickly would warn his kids about the dangers of gambling, he yanked the handle. Then he watched in horror as silver dollars cascaded from the machine. He'd won the jackpot, which was almost three hundred dollars.

The kids exploded in applause, backslaps, and hooting.

"One of my volunteer staff people looked at me and said, 'Your point was…?' "

Tim took the kids to McDonald's for breakfast *and* lunch to get rid of the winnings as quickly as possible.

He couldn't gag the kids, but he wanted them to forget about the jackpot as quickly as possible. "During the rest of the trip, we did some neat things," Tim remembers. He hoped those ministry moments would push the Las Vegas fiasco far back in their thinking. No such luck.

"As soon as the kids piled off the bus in our church parking lot, the first thing out of their mouths was, 'Hey, we went gambling in Vegas and hit the jackpot!' "

Flexibility. It's easy to say but hard to do. And it's an absolute requirement for youth ministry.

"You need to roll with the punches," says Tim. "Don't let your ego be too closely tied to results; you'll get defensive when something doesn't go right." Winning a jackpot, for instance.

What's gone wrong in your ministry? How did you respond? What could you have done to turn it into a learning opportunity?

Stay flexible.

3. HIGH ON JESUS

Larry Lindquist

With his first ministry, Larry inherited a youth choir of nearly two hundred kids. Remembers Larry, "It was incredible to see that many students sharing their love for Christ. Some of them were extraordinarily gifted musicians."

It sounds like instant success, right? Big numbers…big productions…big results…

Not quite.

Larry's group was singing at a community event. The choir had set up an impressive stage with five levels of risers. The tallest guys were in the back row, and their heads almost touched the ceiling.

"As we sang about a changed heart and following Christ, one of the guys in the back row suddenly disappeared. He *really* disappeared."

Larry heard a thud and realized the singer had fallen off the riser. "The other guys on the back row were staring at their friend on the floor. The audience was paying attention to nothing else. I stopped the song and walked around to the back of the risers to see what had happened."

At first Larry thought the boy had fainted, but a closer look confirmed that the boy was high—and not on Jesus.

"I quickly formed an honorable explanation to give the audience, and a volunteer took care of the boy while we finished the program. But, during the rest of the concert, I was thinking about the condition of the student and the hypocrisy of our 'ministry.'"

As he drove back to the church, Larry decided to limit the choir to those who had committed their lives to Christ. Participation wouldn't require perfection, just a sincere commitment.

Larry instantly reduced the group from nearly two hundred to about sixty. "Some of the kids, the

> *"Anyone who lives on milk, being still an infant, is not acquainted with the teaching about righteousness"*
>
> Hebrews 5: 13.

church leadership, and the parents thought I was a total failure and had 'killed' the group," he says.

Congregational meetings and pointed letters followed, but Larry refused to cave. A value about his youth ministry emerged: "I'll only use students in ministry-level opportunities if they give clear testimony of their commitment to Christ."

Let's face it: Nothing impresses church boards more than attendance. Spiritual depth is hard to measure, but packing the pews on "Youth Sunday" makes you an instant hero.

If you've been tempted to set aside building disciples so you could generate numbers, don't do it. Big numbers aren't necessarily a measure of success. Spiritual depth is hard to measure, but it's where discipleship happens.

4. BETTER DEAD THAN RED
Dave Stone

It was Dave Stone's first week at a new church, and he was trying to connect with the kids.

"I had a chance to relate to a little, redheaded seventh-grader," Dave remembers. "His mother was on the board that hired me, so the family was excited about my arrival. He was one of the first kids I went to visit."

Dave remembers walking into the family's home and finding the boy eager and ready to meet him.

"The first thing I said to him was, 'Oh, you're redheaded! Hot dog! I'd rather be dead than red on the head!'"

Dave laughed good-naturedly, then he moved along and met the rest of the family.

> *"The tongue is also a fire, a world of evil among the parts of the body"*
>
> James 3:6a.

"He didn't show up for several weeks, so I finally talked to his mother. I said, 'You know, I haven't seen Randy at church.'"

"She said, 'I've been wanting to tell you about that. You remember when you came to our house?'"

Dave did and told her that normally a visit at home had a *positive* effect.

"She said, 'I think you embarrassed him.'"

Dave couldn't believe it. He'd embarrassed the boy? How?

"She reminded me of what I said about his being a redhead. I didn't even remember what I said," recalls Dave. "I hadn't realized what I'd done. My heart was broken.

"It took me about two years to get Randy back on the team, and I had to *work* at it. He'd been hurt deeply, and my one, little joke did it."

This incident is one reason Dave set a firm rule for his youth group: No put-downs. None. Ever. "I told kids that we're not going to do it in the games we play or in the things we say. I said, 'If we catch someone doing it, we're calling the person on it.' The group became someplace warm to come, someplace you wanted to be. That's why we had kids: It was safe to be there."

How safe is your group? How safe is it for kids who are tall? skinny? fat? smart? held back a grade? who don't agree with you about politics or music?

5. APPEARANCES DO MATTER
Tony Campolo

Tony Campolo was a twenty-one-year-old youth worker at the Mt. Holly Presbyterian Church when he learned something he suggests every youth worker learn early in his or her career.

Says Tony, "I never considered myself a sex object, nor did I believe that I cast any kind of a romantic spell over the teenage girls in my youth group. It was beyond me to think that any of them had romantic designs on me, but I was wrong.

"One Friday evening, the youth group gathered at the church to go bowling. About twenty-five young people piled into cars, and we drove off for a night of recreation. At 10:00 p.m., we wrapped up the bowling and went to a burger place for something to eat. It was about midnight when the whole thing wrapped up and everyone made plans to go home.

"I wasn't aware of the fact that a seventeen-year-old girl in the group had made sure that she was the last one I dropped off. She'd schemed with her friends to be alone with me in the car. Her scheme worked perfectly.

"As we pulled up in front of her house, she said there was something she wanted to talk about with me. I turned off the ignition and waited for her to unburden herself of some spiritual problem or to tell me about some personal crisis. I was all ready to use the limited skills I learned in the Introduction to Psychology class at college; I was prepared to be an expert counselor.

"Avoid every kind of evil"
1 Thessalonians 5:22.

"When she moved over to my side of the car, I realized that she had something else in mind. Once I had things figured out, I asked her to back off, and she did.

"Unfortunately, that wasn't the end of it. Other girls in the group knew what she was up to that evening, and they were all anxious to find out what had happened. Needless to say, she told them things that never took place. It was her way of enhancing her image as a femme fatale. The word got around the school quickly, and I realized my reputation was in serious jeopardy.

"When this girl realized the position I was in, she confessed that she had made up the story. Her repentance became widely known, and I was off the hook.

"I was single at the time, but if I'd been married and if she hadn't confessed that we really had *not* 'made out' in the car that evening, who knows how my life might have turned out?"

Says Tony: "A word to the wise is sufficient. Don't allow yourself to be engineered into being alone with members of your youth group who are of the opposite sex."

How careful are you about this issue? Don't just ask yourself; ask someone else who sees you in action in your ministry.

ALL-STAR ADVICE

Top Ten Things to Never Say After Making a Mistake

10. Really, it's not *that* bad.

9. If you think this was bad, you should hear about the time...

8. The devil made me do it.

7. I can't change the past. Let's focus on the future.

6. Tomorrow nobody will remember.

5. Just giving God a chance to show his redemptive power.

4. Well, nobody's perfect.

3. If nothing else, this can always serve as a bad example.

2. But I *meant* well.

And absolutely, positively never, *ever* say:

1. It seemed like a good idea at the time.

ALL-STAR ADVICE

If Only I'd Known

When you went into youth ministry, someone tagged along—someone who has sabotaged your efforts and set you up for failure—someone who spends way more time than he or she should telling you things that just aren't true.

Hey, Bucky, you've met the enemy, and it's you.

Nothing can stomp your morale flat faster than getting run over by your own expectations.

Here's what several youth ministry pioneers discovered about youth ministry—*after* they were already in the trenches.

Steve Munds: "When I started, the things I taught the kids came out of my personal opinion," remembers Steve. "That's what you preach when you don't have a real knowledge of the Word. Your opinion ministers to those who agree and alienates those who don't agree."

Once he was in ministry full-time, Steve discovered he needed a better grounding in God's Word. "There are no excuses today. There are Bible colleges everywhere that teach both the Word *and* youth ministry."

Dan Jessup: "I thought youth ministry was about kids, but it's not," says Dan. "It's about *people,* and that includes parents and families."

Joani Schultz: Reflecting on her first year in youth ministry, Joani smiles. "You think you're the one who's doing it. What you learn is that you're enabling *other* people to do youth ministry. It's not 'The Joani Show.' Instead, it's me involving kids as leaders and involving parents and grandparents in the ministry."

Les Christie: Growing up in a small church, Les watched a part-time youth minister do everything to pull off the ministry. "So I thought you just did it," Les says. "It wasn't until I'd been in ministry several months that I realized it was just too hard to do alone. I definitely needed other adults. That was the greatest insight I ever had in youth ministry."

THANKS FOR NOTHING

Joani Schultz

Joani Schultz was considering who to recruit to chaperone a youth group winter weekend when her pastor said, "There's this guy who could really benefit from helping out with the retreat. He could use the spiritual lift."

Joani invited the man to come along.

Later Joani discovered the chaperone was selling drugs to the kids.

"It was horrifying to discover how mixed up he was," says Joani. "I understood the pastor's heart in saying that coming on the retreat would lift the guy out of his spiritual doldrums. But it was bad—*really* bad."

Joani discovered the problem while on the retreat, which meant she had to deal with it—and the chaperone—in the middle of the northern woods. She couldn't just send him home.

One kid on the retreat was already struggling with drugs. "To have an adult who planted drugs right there made it hard for him," remembers Joani.

"It was a major learning experience for me: Never, *ever* involve an adult in youth ministry in an attempt to help the adult. You've got to have adults who are solid. Whatever they gain from the kids is dessert."

Joani's experience happened in the days before serious background checks for volunteers. But even a thorough check might not have caught this man's behavior.

How solid are your volunteers in their faith and discipleship? Have you communicated clearly that working with teenagers is a sacred trust with eternal consequences?

Your kids are depending on you, and so are your volunteers.

6. THE HIJACKING OF YFC 474

Scott Larson

When Scott Larson first led a Youth for Christ club, he was still working as a stockbroker.

"It was a tight group of kids," remembers Scott. "There was already a strong leadership, and a few kids were so witty that, week after week, they sort of took the group away from me."

Scott showed up each Monday night prepared to lead, only to have his group hijacked from within. It was a frustrating situation, which he managed to make worse before it got better.

First Scott tried confronting the kids, demanding their respect and attention. "*That* backfired," he says.

"The kids who were feeling sorry for me no longer did. I was the heavy who'd blasted their leaders.

"Meeting with the leaders individually worked a lot better. I said, 'I really need you to help me. As you can see, I have no control over this group,'" admits Scott.

Scott eventually built relationships with the group's leaders. "As they began to respect me, they started to move the group *with* me instead of *against* me," he says.

Any youth leader who walks into an existing group risks stepping on the land mines Scott found. "Some leaders in a group feel it's their job to protect the group from new leaders," warns Scott. "Figure out who the leaders are. They're probably *not* the adults."

The good news: A number of the kids in that first, frustrating group still stay in touch with Scott, and a surprising number of them wound up in ministry.

Who are the natural leaders in your group? Are they working with you—or against you? Why? How could you improve your partnership?

And While You're at It, God...

At church staff meetings, Jim Kochenburger's senior pastor gave updates on illnesses and deaths in the congregation. One week, when Jim wasn't paying close enough attention, he prayed for God to heal a guy the pastor had just announced was dead.

"*That* impressed everyone," says Jim.

7. THE NON-RETURN OF THE PRODIGAL SONS

Rick Lawrence

For most of the urban kids Rick Lawrence and his partners led into the Colorado mountains, this hike was their first. The kids were campers at a Christian ranch that caters to low-income, inner-city kids, and Rick was a counselor.

"These were kids who'd seldom left the city, and they had absolutely no idea what they were doing," remembers Rick. "They had exactly no hiking or camping experience."

The hike went along well—at first. New sights and sounds kept kids occupied. Eventually blisters and backpacks that seemed increasingly heavy took their toll. Some kids lagged behind. Others became argumentative.

About ten miles into the excursion, two kids were so negative that Rick and the other adults delivered an ultimatum: Either get with the program, or turn around and go home.

"Fine," the two kids said. They turned around and stomped off.

Rick and his group sat down to wait for the return of the repentant prodigals. They were smug and confident that the kids would quickly return since the sun was slipping behind a distant ridge. They waited for ten minutes…twenty minutes…half an hour.

"That's when we realized that they weren't coming back," remembers Rick. "They didn't have the faintest clue how to get through a night in the wilderness, and we'd let them walk off alone. They were in real danger."

The adults and remaining kids quickly turned around and set off after the wayward pair. "We backtracked, but didn't find anything," says Rick. When it was too dark to continue, the group of hikers made camp to wait out the night.

"Nobody got a lot of sleep," recalls Rick.

The next day Rick and his group found the two renegade hikers. They'd spent the night next to some railroad tracks.

Because of the time it took to chase down the two kids, the whole group had to return to camp.

"I learned that you can't threaten with a consequence you're not prepared to follow through on," says Rick. The adults had given the kids a choice, and the kids had selected one of the options. "It just wasn't an option we were really prepared to let them take," says Rick.

What about the consequences you present to your kids? Are you really going to turn the church bus around and cancel the fall retreat unless everyone settles down?

Listen to yourself when you're in conflict with your kids. Are you being clear, concise, and consistent? Do you follow through with what you say you'll do?

8. HELLO? ANYONE OUT THERE?

Larry Acosta

As a young youth worker in California back in 1985, Larry Acosta put together a major outreach event for his youth group.

He organized a Friday-night-to-Saturday-morning evangelism training workshop for his kids, then charged them with bringing friends to a concert Saturday evening.

"I brought in a band for this big concert where we'd share the gospel with unchurched students," remembers Larry, who made sure they were ready for a blowout crowd.

As it happened, that crowd never showed up.

"That night we had just a few more kids than our normal youth group," says Larry. "It was definitely a failure if you judged by the numbers. The number of kids who came didn't justify the amount of money invested."

Larry felt humiliated because the band's lead singer was a good friend.

"I just had to suck it up while I helped the band pack everything up and haul it out to the van. Then I went back to my office, knelt down, and confessed to the Lord that it had been too much about me. I needed big numbers of kids that night to prove my effectiveness as a youth worker.

"In a huge state of brokenness, I told the Lord that, if he'd show me how to do youth ministry his way, I'd do it with healthier motives and in a way that was more pleasing to him."

Larry got up from his knees with a new perspective on youth ministry.

"We started a discipleship program to disciple kids," he says. "I'd brought my kids in for a little training and then sent them out to bring back their unchurched friends. But they weren't discipled. They weren't ready.

"What came out of this experience was my learning the priority of Biblical youth ministry: Through discipleship you take kids deeper with the Lord. You do the deeper things that take more time instead of the superficial things—like the dog-and-pony entertainment-driven thing—that may be easier."

Are you creating disciples in your youth ministry? If so, how?

Write the names of five kids in your group below. What's your plan to help them grow in their discipleship?

_____

_____

_____

9. ALL I AM SAYING IS: GIVE THOM A CHANCE
Thom Schultz

Thom Schultz started in youth ministry during the era of the Vietnam War and antiwar demonstrations.

"On one occasion, we took our group to perform a play at a church in Boulder, Colorado," remembers Thom.

At that time, the University of Colorado in Boulder was known as Berkeley East because of its frequent, often violent, campus protests.

Thom's group finished the performance and piled into cars for the drive home. When Thom switched on the radio, he heard that an antiwar protest on campus had escalated into a full-fledged riot.

Being an adventuresome sort, Thom thought the kids might benefit from seeing a bit of news in the making. "I turned to the three kids in my car and asked, 'Want to go to a riot?'

"Being high school and junior high kids, they answered, 'Sure!'"

Thom drove to the campus, and the foursome got out to walk around. Unfortunately, at precisely that moment, the riot changed directions, and came right at them.

"The kids got tear-gassed," says Thom, who managed to push the kids into his car and drive out of the area without further incident.

By the time the kids got home and related the story to their parents, the story had grown. The guys said they'd almost been killed, and the girl said she'd almost been raped.

"I was in *big* trouble," says Thom, who had to explain what he was thinking to several people, including the senior pastor.

Thom survived his mishap by admitting he'd been wrong.

"This was one of those things there's just flat-out no excuse for," he says. "I acknowledged I was wrong, said I was sorry, and asked for forgiveness. Then I called each of the parents and said the same thing."

When you blow it, what people like to hear is that you're sorry and you've learned something.

It takes humility and a willingness to be teachable.

When's the last time you apologized for something you said or did? When's the last time you *needed* to?

ALL-STAR ADVICE

Our Friend the Mistake

A sad fact: You seldom make progress without making mistakes.

The trick is to make *smart* mistakes—mistakes that move you ahead and teach you something as you go.

Here are five ideas to help you along the journey:

If possible, make mistakes in *theory*, not practice.

Scientists often create models of experiments prior to actually mixing chemicals or lining up lab rats. Fatal flaws in programs can often be predicted if your first step is sitting down and thinking through an entire event, piece by piece.

Do your homework.

Keep a journal of what you did at retreats and programs and how your kids reacted. Maintain a file on each of your volunteers, including your take on the volunteer's weaknesses, strengths, and plans for development. The more you learn from experience, the better you'll be able to predict how kids and volunteers will react to your new ideas and situations.

Pay special attention to documenting plans that flop; it's from those plans you can *really* learn.

Don't hide mistakes—from yourself or others.

The youth leaders who contributed to this book did you a huge favor: They didn't pretend their ministries were a long string of uninterrupted successes. That lets you benefit from what they learned. Be as quick to share your mistakes as your successes at the next youth workers conference you attend.

And don't deny to *yourself* that you goofed.

When a program bombs, your first reactions will be embarrassment and anger (see Duffy Robbins' story on page 49). But, if you acquire the ability to learn from mistakes, you'll find you make fewer of them. Become excellent at identifying where you made a critical error. Until you do, you're sure to repeat it.

Build safety nets.

Become a fanatic about having a Plan B up your sleeve. What happens to your ski trip if there's no snow? to the picnic if it rains? if a kid gets hurt? Backup plans and safety nets help you keep "situations" from becoming "mistakes." Be a good scout: Expect the unexpected and be prepared.

Contingency plans are like spare tires: You seldom need them, but you'll feel better knowing they're there. And you'll learn to think strategically as you develop backup plans.

Ask yourself: How great is the risk?

OK, you've got a great idea. And, if you want a truly life-changing youth ministry, you need to take some risks. But be sure the risks you take are *calculated* risks. If making a mistake will endanger your ministry's credibility or someone's safety (for instance, taking kids on an overnight into the backcountry when you've never been back-packing yourself), proceeding is foolhardy.

Save your risk-taking for the small stuff that doesn't really matter.

10. HOW TO BUILD A NEW CHURCH DOOR

Walt Mueller

Walt Mueller was once asked by four of his more responsible high school kids to loan them his church key.

"They were working on a float, which our youth group would enter in a parade," Walt remembers. He had to teach a Bible study elsewhere, so, after cautioning the kids to be responsible, Walt handed over his key.

After working on the float awhile, the kids realized they needed supplies from the hardware store. "One of the girls in the group was the senior pastor's daughter," says Walt. "And one of the guys, who wasn't old enough to drive, talked her into letting him stick the ignition key in her dad's pickup truck and turn over the engine."

Not knowing how to drive, the boy didn't realize that the truck was a stick shift and that it had been left in gear. When the engine roared into life, so did the rest of the truck.

"While he was turning the key, the truck was hopping forward *real* fast, with *lots* of power," says Walt. "He panicked."

The pastor's truck crashed into the church building, ripping a hole clear through the wall.

"One of the kids called me and said there was a problem," says Walt, who excused himself from the Bible study and rushed to church. "The girl was sitting in a dark Sunday school classroom, praying that her father wouldn't kill her. And the guy was so upset that he was kneeling in front of the communion rail, crying."

Disasters and interruptions of *all* sizes come with the territory when you're in youth ministry. Most of them happen when you need to be doing something else.

How well do you handle the unexpected? the intrusive? Is it a threat, an aggravation, or perhaps the hand of God working?

SHORT SCREW-UP

Hypocrites Welcome!

When Dave Stone was asked to place ads in local high school annuals, he agreed. His ad read, "Welcome, hypocrites! First United Methodist Youth Ministry. The perfect, beware."

Dave's intent was to let kids know his youth group was a safe place for imperfect people to visit.

Dave caught a *lot* of flack from the conservative members of his church, especially when he planted a sign with the same message outside the youth building. Was *this* the image the church wanted? Were *these* the sort of kids the church wanted to attract? What was he *thinking*?

"But," says Dave, "When our youth group grew from 50 to 350 in a few years, I could do whatever I wanted to."

11. MY KINGDOM FOR A NAME TAG
Mike Nappa

As the assistant junior high pastor in a large Southern California church, Mike Nappa was used to seeing visitors. And he was intentional about connecting with them.

"I was determined to greet them all," he remembers.

One evening, he spotted a little guy standing alone while the rest of the kids shouted, played, and drew pictures on a white board.

Intent on making the guy feel at home, Mike made his way across the room and planted himself in front of the wallflower.

"Hi," said Mike. "I don't remember seeing you before. Is this your first time here?"

"The guy looked at me, puzzled," remembers Mike. "He said, 'Actually, I've been attending for three months now. In fact, you just wrote me a letter this week telling me how you were glad I was coming.'

"I struggled to regain my composure. I said, 'Oh, yeah! Right! You're Brian, aren't you?'

" 'No. My name is Jeff,' he said. Then he went to join some friends who'd just arrived. I wanted to go soak my head in the toilet."

Ouch.

Forgetting a student's name is bad enough. But forgetting a *student*? So much for building self-esteem.

But it happens: We forget kids, miss birthdays, and lose track of who's dating whom. Letting facts central to our kids' world escape us hurts our ministries.

What sort of record-keeping do you have in place to help you stay on top of names, dates, and faces? Paperwork may be boring, but when it helps you be more effective, it's worth the pain.

12. JESUS SAVES WHAT?
Jim Kochenburger

It had been a great youth group day-trip. Warm water under clear skies made Pine Lake ideal for swimming.

As Jim Kochenburger drove the church bus home, with worship

music blasting, he thanked God for a wonderful time of enjoying nature with his youth group.

Other drivers were enjoying nature too, as Jim discovered a few hours later.

"In the back of the bus, three guys—including one of my student leaders—were pressing their bare bottoms against the glass right above the words 'Jesus Saves,' " remembers Jim. "I didn't have a clue until we were back home."

That's when the associate pastor—a former youth leader—roared into sight and cornered Jim. "His son was on the bus, and he was fired up. He walked up to me yelling, 'You've got to do something! You've got to lay down the law!' "

So Jim found the bare-bottom ringleader and lit into him. "I really let him have it," said Jim, who called down significant amounts of fire and brimstone.

Later, Jim realized his motive for disciplining the teenager had been all wrong. "I had to go back and apologize because my motivations were so poor. It wasn't about his actions. It was about my looking bad in front of the associate pastor."

"I learned two valuable lessons," says Jim. "First, always put an adult in the back of the bus. Second, think through your motivations before you act."

We hate to look bad, especially in front of key people. But if we're not careful, we can become more concerned about pleasing them than pleasing God.

Whose opinions matter most when you're shaping your youth ministry? Why?

CHANGES? WE DON'T NEED NO STINKIN' CHANGES!

Darrell Pearson

Darrell Pearson spent eleven years at a church, nine as a junior high pastor and two as the senior high pastor.

"One of the smartest things I did was *not* change anything my first year," remembers Darrell. "I just ran my predecessor's junior high program, which about killed me because there were things I didn't like at all.

"By the time the year was up, I realized some of the things I didn't like were really intelligent things to do. I just hadn't seen the wisdom in them."

Darrell especially recalls how the previous leader had set up separate retreats for sixth-graders, seventh-graders, and eighth-graders. "It was a really smart thing to do," says Darrell, who points out that a structure set up in 1978 is still being used—because it works.

His experience prompted Darrell to advise other workers repeatedly to give it a year before trying to change much. He suggests using that twelve months to listen and learn.

"Here's where my mistake comes in," says Darrell. "After nine years as junior high pastor, I took over the senior high spot. And I completely *didn't* pay attention to my own advice."

He already knew most of the kids. He knew the church. So Darrell immediately revamped everything he thought should change, expecting kids to jump on board eagerly. It didn't happen.

"I bombed the first fall," Darrell recalls. "In print the program looked great, but we couldn't pull it off. It was a disaster."

When you move into a new ministry setting, it's tempting to immediately make a mark and signal a new, improved regime. You want to incorporate all the great stuff you've used before. You want to eliminate stale, "we've always done it this way" programming.

Resist the temptation.

"You can *add* some things, but don't take anything away," says Darrell. "A year seems like forever, but what's in place is sometimes better than you think."

When you make changes in your program, ask yourself why. Are you trying to embrace the latest trend? responding to kids' suggestions? or listening for the leading of God?

13. VICE NIGHT
Monty Hipp

While serving in his first youth ministry at a Seattle area church, Monty Hipp organized theme-night outreach events.

The idea was to pick up on a popular TV show, print tickets, and then have kids invite their friends. It was a great concept and well-received—until Monty did a *Miami Vice* night.

"We had the music, the leisure jackets, the whole thing," he remembers.

"A parent called me Wednesday afternoon before the event. Then, because of his concerns about the *Miami Vice* theme, the parent called about twenty *other* parents.

"He said, 'I understand everyone is supposed to get dressed up. But all the girls on *Miami Vice* are hookers. So what should my daughter dress up like?'"

Monty quickly discovered that this one parent's concerned phone calls had started a rumor that Monty was

> *"Be completely humble and gentle; be patient, bearing with one another in love"*
>
> Ephesians 4:2

promoting prostitution and girls dressing loosely.

It didn't help Monty's cause that parents dropping off their kids at the event saw kids munching candy cigarettes, a prop Monty thought would add to the fun.

"We saw thirty-eight kids come to Christ that night, but thirty-eight families threatened to leave the church. So it was basically a wash," says Monty.

Communicating with parents can be tremendously frustrating. It sometimes seems that, no matter what you do to keep them informed, you never hear from parents until they're upset. Then they call everyone but you.

How do you deal with parents who are quick to second-guess you? who undermine your ministry? who seem intent on "getting" you?

ALL-STAR ADVICE

How to Survive a Board Meeting

OK, you screwed up…big time. You're at the top of the board meeting agenda, and a few of the guys look like they'd love to use you for target practice.

How will you get through this alive?

Don't make excuses. If it was your responsibility, say so. If it was your mistake, own it. Nobody likes a finger-pointer who blames others and won't admit an error in judgement.

Do be professional. *Everyone* makes mistakes. Doctors, lawyers, and convenience-store clerks all make mistakes. Nobody expects you to be perfect, but it's reasonable to expect you to take the consequences and fix what you break—if it's fixable.

Don't compare. Saying your mistake isn't as bad as the one the senior pastor made won't make any friends anywhere. Stick to the issue at hand.

Don't resort to humor. Maybe the church bus breaking down because you forgot to add oil *will* be something you'll all laugh about in ten years. Nobody is laughing now.

Don't offer to resign. If the board wants you gone, you'll soon know it. The time to make a grand gesture isn't when you're feeling bad about yourself or when you've just nose-dived professionally. Give it a month, then see if you still want to make the offer.

Get over it. The sooner you put the mistake behind you, the quicker everyone else will too.

The board meeting is *not* about you? Great! Here are four tips from Jim Kochenburger to keep it that way:

Take minutes. It'll keep you awake, and remind you when a decision needs to be made. You can keep your items from being tabled.

Strategically engage board members *before* the meeting. What people don't know about you and your ministry can and will hurt you.

Don't speak "kid" to grown-ups. Keep your appearance and demeanor appropriate. Give details. Be brief and to the point.

Gently see if your presence is *really* necessary. If your only function is to give a three-minute report at the end of the meeting, suggest you be moved to the front end of the meeting. After your report, excuse yourself to go do ministry.

14. FOLLOW THE LEADER
Ron Luce

As he launched Teen Mania, Ron Luce threw himself into the ministry with passion and conviction.

Unfortunately, neither was enough.

Ron quickly discovered there was a missing component: leadership.

"I almost wrecked Teen Mania because of it," recalls Ron.

Like most youth ministries, Teen Mania had attracted people who were dedicated to the cause but were not necessarily skilled in key leadership roles. "I didn't know how to be a leader," says Ron. "All I knew was that I wanted to reach a lot of kids and I wanted to change the world."

The result: Even as Teen Mania developed a reputation for great programming, it was falling apart internally. "We had great conferences; we had kids going on missions trips. Yet people hated working at Teen Mania. *I* hated working at Teen Mania," says Ron.

The solution was for Ron to gain the leadership abilities he lacked, from handling finances, delegating, and creating job descriptions to selecting and training other leaders and planning. Ron needed to grow in these areas to take Teen Mania to the next level.

"You've got to keep growing as a leader," says Ron, who suggests that youth workers get acquainted with the "Business" section of the local bookstore.

"We're in the life business—the business of touching young people's hearts. There is a business component to it. It's not a sin to think about the business side, so let's get some business savvy."

Ron quickly points out that there's a difference between growing as a Christian and growing as a leader. "People think 'I'm going to get

> *"For by the grace given me I say to every one of you: Do not think of yourself more highly than you ought, but rather think of yourself with sober judgment, in accordance with the measure of faith God has given you"*
>
> Romans 12:3.

closer to God, and then I'll reach more people.' That's not necessarily true. You'll probably be more on fire and may be able to reach people in a deeper, more profound way, but you may not reach *more* people.

"You have to grow as a leader if you're going to broaden your impact and reach more people. As you grow as a leader, your group will grow.

"Don't prioritize growing as a leader over your walk with God, but leadership growth ought to be second in line," suggests Ron, who has this to say of his first years in youth ministry: "I wish I had learned that I needed to grow as a leader."

Leadership. About a million books about leadership are on the shelves, but what's the bottom line for youth ministry?

Here's what Ron has to say about your role as a leader in ministry:

"Youth ministers who have passion—and *only* passion—will eventually burn themselves out. Passion only grows your ministry to a certain level. You'll find you're peddling faster and faster to reach more kids only to discover you don't know your spouse and kids any longer. So you think, 'Well, I have to quit the youth ministry.' If you grow as a leader, you'll compliment your passion with wisdom about how to use your passion for the biggest impact."

Ask three adults who have a clear view of your ministry to tell you how you're doing as a leader. What are your strengths and your weaknesses? What will you do to grow this year?

15. SQUARE PEGS AND ROUND HOLES
Karen Dockrey

Do you think veteran youth workers never make mistakes? Think again.

"I've been in youth ministry twenty-eight years, and I've just become aware of this problem in the past three years," says Karen

Dockrey, who confesses she's been as guilty as the next youth worker.

Call it spiritual snobbery.

"We don't intend to do it, but we develop a spiritual hierarchy," says Karen. "We value some gifts and temperaments more than others."

Here's how it works: Susan is outgoing and talkative, and you decide she's a "leader." So you affirm Susan whenever she shows glimmers of leadership. You give her tasks and challenges that develop her leadership skills and give her visibility in the group. When she answers a question or makes a comment, you take her seriously.

Then there's Frank. He comes just as often and answers just as frequently, but because he's quiet and introverted, you consider him a "follower." When he answers, you give him a cursory nod, if that. You want to know what Susan will say.

Yet, if you looked carefully at Frank's life, you'd find he consistently expresses his gift of encouragement, and he does it well. At home, at school, and throughout his life, he's serving Christ with a quiet zeal that doesn't stand out at youth group.

So you dismiss Frank's occasional comments at youth group. You pass him over for an upfront role at the fall retreat. And soon you've driven Frank away—and convinced him to stop serving.

Do you see what happened? Your prophesy was fulfilled as Susan become a leader and Frank faded from sight.

Karen has seen situations in which a leader pushed away several kids who were genuine servants in favor of a "pseudo-leader"—a student who was popular but had no spiritual depth.

"He could give the 'churchy' answer, the kind that pleases teachers, when asked how God was leading his life, but he was aloof in his relationships." This same kid who was pegged for leadership at church was destructive at school.

> "The body is a unit, though it is made up of many parts; and though all its parts are many, they form one body. So it is with Christ"
>
> 1 Corinthians 12:12.

"The literature says to look for leaders and to look for the core group—the ones we identify as our 'spiritual' kids. But the Bible says everyone is equal at the foot of the cross," warns Karen. "Everyone has a spiritual gift. When we identify our favorite kids—the ones who do things *our* way—as the 'spiritual' ones, we can drive equally spiritual kids and spiritually deeper kids away from the church and from God. We also give kids a lopsided view of what youth groups—and the church—are all about."

"The big mistake is to value one person over another. The solution is to overtly value everyone's contribution."

Says Karen, "When we value only certain kids, we work against the growth of all youth. And we destroy at least some of them."

We all have favorite kids. We try to keep it from showing, but kids quickly figure it out.

Do you value every person in your youth ministry? Really? What have you said or done to communicate that?

List the names of kids in your group—kids with whom you have contact and influence. Next to each name write something you see God doing in and through that kid's life.

In the next ten days, tell each individual what you've written. You'll revolutionize your youth group.

16. WHAT? ME WORRY?
Andy Hansen

Andy Hansen's first youth group wasn't large, and the church didn't have vans and buses for road trips.

"To get the group anywhere, parents had to drive," says Andy.

No adults wanted to haul kids to a Saturday event at a Bible college a few hours away. "But a church family allowed me to drive the family station wagon," remembers Andy.

After a late start, Andy was determined to make up a little time. "I was probably going ten miles an hour over the speed limit," he admits. "I noticed a red dash light come on. It said something about 'engine warning,' but I knew we were about five miles from an exit. I figured I'd get off at that exit and find a gas station."

Two miles later, a screeching noise was followed by a death rattle. "I barely lurched off the road. There was steam coming out everywhere." Andy had blown the engine.

After phoning the college to come get his kids, he had to call the station wagon's owners. "I told them I didn't have a car anymore—and neither did they. And I needed another one to get home."

At the next board meeting, the question was raised about what to do for the owners of the car that had been blown up by the youth minister.

> *"Whatever you do, work at it with all your heart, as working for the Lord, not for men, since you know that you will receive an inheritance from the Lord as a reward. It is the Lord Christ you are serving"*
>
> Colossians 3:23-24.

"The debate about what was fair lasted about half an hour. The discussion included the comment that, 'Well, Andy blew up the engine. Do we dock his pay? What do you think?' Finally the board voted to replace the engine; it wasn't deducted from my pay."

Cutting corners.

Whether it's speeding, not really preparing for a lesson, or failing to make good on a promise to your kids, it's bound to catch you.

In what ways is your ministry notable because of excellence?

17. LISTEN UP
John Cutshall

John Cutshall was in the middle of a youth group meeting when he almost ended his marriage.

"I was standing up front in my glory, expounding on the Word of God in ways that would make Paul proud, when I looked in the back of the room and saw my wife talking to one of the teenage girls," he remembers.

At that point, John could have assumed she was affirming a student who needed a friend, sharing the gospel, or offering a wise word of counsel.

He didn't do any of those.

Instead, says John, "I called her name and said, 'Listen up!'"

He completed the lesson and gave an invitation.

It was very shortly thereafter that John's wife (whom he describes, in anticipation of her reading this, as lovely and completely, totally *right*) informed him that she was not a member of his youth group and henceforth was to be treated with the respect due a lifelong partner.

"The correct answer to that sort of comment is: 'Yes. You're right. Forgive me,'" says John, who said just that.

"The incorrect answer is anything else," suggests John, who said he knew a youth worker who was in a similar situation and told his offended wife, "Then quit acting like one."

"He's still able to walk," says John. "That amazes me."

How do you treat your spouse when your students are around?

If you're married, your marriage can be a solid model of what a fun, Christ-centered, purposeful marriage looks like…if that's what you have.

How's your marriage doing? And how does your spouse feel about your ministry and his or her role in it?

18. THE MISSING MENTOR

Randy Matthews

In 1971, when Randy Matthews became the youth pastor of a Cincinnati church, the youth culture was in a midst of tremendous shift.

"It was right at the height of hippie-dom," remembers Randy, who was soon to earn a national reputation in Christian music.

Randy had been at the church just a short while when he started hosting "Bible Raps."

"We just opened up the church sanctuary on Saturday nights, and kids showed up. And it was a *big* crowd," says Randy. "All we did was talk about the Bible, and then I'd ask a couple questions."

The Bible Raps quickly outgrew the church space, and Randy wanted a more suitable spot for counterculture kids to meet. "We came across an old house nearby, and that's how the 'Jesus House' got started."

Randy and his team turned the first floor of the rambling, two-story mansion into a concert space that held several hundred people, as long as they didn't mind sitting on the floor. The upstairs rooms became bedrooms and meeting rooms for Randy and his small staff.

The Jesus House and the conservative, suburban church that was bankrolling the project were not what you'd call a perfect match.

"The church was supportive of what we were doing," remembers Randy, "but they were kind of stand-offish, too."

"Let the wise listen and add to their learning, and let the discerning get guidance…"

Proverbs 1:5.

Still, it could have been worse. "The pastor was very supportive. I suspect he took a lot of heat that I didn't know about," says Randy.

Having someone in the church champion his youth ministry's cause was important, Randy remembers, and he regrets not doing a better job of making it happen.

"We could have avoided a lot of misunderstandings and communication breakdowns if we'd had an older counsel with us," he says. "We didn't need someone dictating what we could do. What we needed was an older, father-figure type to work with us. Someone from the church with whom we could have worked more closely and had more contact could have helped."

A champion—someone who understands what you're doing and will bridge the gap to the church board. Who wouldn't want someone like that on board?

But notice Randy also suggested that this person would provide *counsel*.

We all want to be understood; that's a given. But only the wisest of us also seek to be understanding of others.

What are you doing to better understand your church board? your pastor?

ALL-STAR ADVICE

How to Last in Youth Ministry

They go together like peanut butter and jelly…milk and cookies…or bread and butter: Youth ministry and lock-ins.

You know the drill. You and *way* too many kids gather in a confined space that's big enough for games, devotions, games, snacks, and games—but no sleep.

Barry St. Clair remembers his first lock-in, and he remembers a promise he made to himself when it ended.

"The first lock-in I did was a tremendous success," says Barry. "We'd been involved with the kids for a year and a half, visiting their campus, discipling kids, and meeting with them every week. We had great relationships, so kids were bringing their friends.

"At the lock-in, we had kids all *over* the place. I don't know about the spiritual value, but it was a night of incredible fun. It was also exhausting; it took a week to recover.

"I was so proud of myself for getting through it that I said, 'That's it. Last one. I will not do a lock-in for the rest of my ministry.'

"I've kept that promise," says Barry. "I won't sponsor one, and I'll never speak at one. I've kept that promise to myself over all these years, and it's been a really, really good thing.

"I will attest to the fact that a key to my longevity in youth ministry is that I quit doing lock-ins early on. They cost you *big* time."

Whether it's not being able to pull all-nighters or your inability to survive a week of wilderness camping, it's no sin to work within your boundaries. It's called "knowing your limitations."

Are there boundaries you'd be smart to respect? What are they? Have you been too proud to admit they're there?

19. "DOOOOUG!"
Doug Herman

It was Doug Herman's first weekend at a Colorado church—a great time for a "get to know you" trip with the kids. So Doug took his youth group backpacking at St. Mary's Glacier.

Having heard it was possible to sled down the glacier, Doug's group brought along trash bags. Once they reached the top of the glacier, kids pulled trash bags over their lower bodies and formed trains by sitting in single file and grabbing each other's waists.

"One girl, Tracy, was with me in the first little train," remembers Doug. "It went fine until we got to a place where the glacier was getting really steep."

What Doug didn't know was that the incline became almost vertical at the bottom.

"We were sliding down in the snow, going faster and faster. I dug my elbows in to stop us. I told John, another kid in the train, to go back and warn everyone else that it was too steep."

John did as he was told. As Tracy stood up, with her feet wrapped in plastic, she slipped.

"She was sliding on her belly, digging her fingernails into the snow. And she was screaming 'Dooooug!' as she went over the cliff."

Doug could see people at the bottom staring then running toward the place the sound had stopped. He pulled off his plastic and got down the glacier as fast as he could—where he found that Tracy had fractured her ankle.

"We had to carry her out," remembers Doug.

He'll always remember hearing the girl shouting his name as she disappeared from sight. "That'll be with me forever," says Doug.

Scouting ahead to check terrain is a good idea—*always*—but it's something we often fail to do.

It's one thing to trust God to care for the kids in your care. It's another thing to not do your homework.

Does the preparation you do for events communicate that you care about your kids? that you value their safety and well-being? How would your kids and their parents answer that question?

20. BEACH BLANKET BOZO
Duffy Robbins

Duffy Robbins remembers a 50s theme night his youth group held back in the 80s.

They had it all: 50s games, 50s dress, 50s music, and the ultimate idea: "We planned to show *Beach Blanket Bingo*—backward."

The first half of the event went well. Nearly two hundred kids filled a gym located across a parking lot from the church. By the time he was due to show the movie, Duffy knew he was on a roll. "I was thinking, 'Duffy, you are a *genius*,'" he remembers.

The time came for Duffy to start the film. After lining kids up facing a gym wall as if they were at a drive-in and dimming the lights, he threw the switch…and got nothing.

"Remember that this was *before* videos," says Duffy. "We had 16 mm projectors, which were also known as instruments of Satan. They were a complicated mess of gears, so it wasn't unusual to start a film and then have to turn the lights back on to fix something."

What Duffy didn't know was that, after being tested in the warm church, the bulb didn't survive the trip across a frozen parking lot in January.

> "And we know that in all things God works for the good of those who love him, who have been called according to his purpose"
>
> Romans 8:28.

"About the fourth time I had the lights turned off and on again, I was feeling the pressure. I was nervous and embarrassed. The kids were staring at me. I was mad at the church for making me use such antiquated equipment, and I was mad at God. I mean, why didn't he just heal the thing? Didn't he know we needed to watch *Beach Blanket Bingo* backward so kids could come to Christ?"

And that's when it happened. "Some kid yelled out, 'We want our money back!'"

Duffy went over the edge. "I yelled, 'Everybody up against the wall!' My kids had never heard me yell like that before, so they all got up and went. I was furious, and I launched into a ten-minute rant against them. I used manipulation and guilt; I told them they'd hurt my feelings. My benediction was, 'This night is over. Go home. Goodbye.'"

Slowly the kids gathered up their things and filed out into the January night. In just a few minutes Duffy was standing alone in a very large, very empty gym. It held just him and a broken-bulbed projector.

"I didn't even go back to the church," Duffy recalls. "I walked home and lay in bed thinking, 'What will I do next?'"

A perfect evening turned into a disaster in just minutes.

A few days later Duffy received a postcard from a girl in his youth group. "She wrote, 'I'm sorry we hurt your feelings. When I saw how mad you got, I knew how much you must care. I knew how much you love us. Then I realized how much *God* must love us. I'll never forget this night.'"

Duffy still has the card.

Says Duffy, "What I learned from this experience is that God can take all the negatives—including me losing my temper—add them up and come out with a positive."

Try as you might, you'll never be perfect, and neither will your ministry. When something or someone disappoints you—even when the someone is yourself—will you be forgiving? Will you let God work through even your failures?

21. WHO LOVES YOU, BABY?
Steve Munds

When Steve Munds started in youth ministry, nobody quite knew what "youth ministry" *meant*.

"Youth ministry lacked its own identity," remembers Steve. "So you had to crawl and scratch to get what you needed. It was easy to develop the mentality that nobody cared about the kids as much as you did—not even the pastor."

Steve says he fell victim to an attitude of "spiritual insubordination," and it was the biggest mistake of his early youth ministry. Though he never openly voiced his feelings to the kids, the leaders picked up on his attitude and passed it along through the ranks.

"The youth ministry became its own entity. The pastor was frustrated because kids weren't sticking. The kids grew up with the mentality that the church wasn't there for them. *Steve* was there for them. The *youth ministry* was there for them, but the *church* wasn't there for them.

> "Instead, speaking the truth in love, we will in all things grow up into him who is the Head, that is, Christ"
>
> Ephesians 4:15.

"Youth pastors have to realize that youth ministry is not an entity in itself. You're here because of the church. The church is not here because of you. That's something that I had to learn."

Here's the litmus test: How well do kids transition out of your ministry into the larger ministry of the church?

If kids graduate from the youth room and then disappear, why? Is anything *you're* doing encouraging them to doubt that the church will meet their needs?

22. NO PROBLEM
Les Christie

A few months after Les Christie went on staff at Eastside Christian Church, an adult volunteer named Al suggested they take the youth group water-skiing.

"I'd never been water-skiing," says Les, "but Al had a station wagon and boat, so I said, 'Sure.' "

When they got to the lake, Al asked Les to back the station wagon up so Al could get the boat in the water. "I'd never done that before either, but I agreed," remembers Les.

That's when problems developed.

While the station wagon was backing up, the boat trailer began to jackknife. Al signaled for Les to turn one way and then the other, but still the boat wasn't where it needed to be. If only they could get the trailer a few inches further into the lake, the boat would float.

"At this point the station wagon's back wheels were in the water, but Al kept signaling me to back up. So I kept backing up.

"I ended up backing the car so far into the water that it began to float," says Les. It didn't float long, though. As water cascaded into the station wagon, Les had to swim out the window to safety.

Al eventually had to sell the car because it smelled so bad.

After less than three months at a church, Les had destroyed a sponsor's car. That has to be some sort of a record.

The good news: "For eight years, Al continued to be a sponsor. He didn't get mad, and he hung in there with me." The bad news: "Al was *always* telling that story. And it didn't do much to build my credibility with the youth group."

Be careful about taking on tasks you don't know how to complete. It may be a clear sign that it's someone else's ministry to do—or that you shouldn't go there at all.

23. THE THIRTEENTH NIGHT
Dave Stone

It was a novel idea: Let a team of kids and leaders create a portable youth rally and take it from town to town.

Dave Stone decided to give it a try, and soon he and the Youth Caravan Team embarked on a very ambitious tour.

"We stopped in fifteen cities during a three-week period, and every night we held a Reach Out Service," remembers Dave. "We invited kids to come forward to kneel at the altar and stay as long as they wanted to stay. Those with prayer requests could simply lift a hand and one of our team members would come to pray with them. We did it every night."

At the thirteenth city, Dave was surprised to see one of the kids kneeling at the altar was Sherwood, a student he'd brought along to minister to peers.

"Keep in mind that I didn't have thirteen talks," says Dave. "The kids on our team had heard my same talk every night, night after night."

Dave approached Sherwood and knelt next to him. "I asked him if he had a prayer request. He said, 'I don't know what made you say it tonight, but I heard what you said. I want to give my heart to the Lord in a different way than I ever have.'

> "He has showed you, O man, what is good. And what does the LORD require of you? To act justly and to love mercy and to walk humbly with your God"
>
> Micah 6:8.

"I didn't say it aloud, but I was thinking, 'Sherwood, where have you *been*? I've been saying the same thing every night!'"

Dave chuckles as he tells the story. "Sherwood just didn't hear it until the thirteenth night.

"That's why, every chance I get, I say that we aren't called to be successful—we're called to be faithful. We need to trust God for the success. Success may not happen while we're still at a church or even in our lifetime, but we're called to keep planting those seeds."

How do you measure success? by numbers? impact? hours worked? kids converted?

What would happen if you gave up trying to be successful and focused on being faithful? How would that change your ministry? your kids? yourself?

ALL-STAR ADVICE

Make the Church Custodian Your Friend

Early on in his career, Darrell Pearson learned that the one person he absolutely, positively *had* to have on his side was the church custodian.

"I worked really hard to know the custodians," remembers Darrell, who fires off a list of reasons you must be on good terms with whoever sweeps the floors.

For starters, many custodians do more than it appears. "One guy in particular had been a Bible-college student," recalls Darrell, who watched how the man worked with people in the church, encouraging them in their ministries. "He truly was a pastor without being recognized as such."

Custodians may clean toilets, but they're fellow staff members. Respect them and their service role. Insist your kids do the same.

Remember: Custodians critique your ministry. If they complain to their boss, who is often the church administrator, that you're leaving giant youth ministry messes to clean up, you'll get a visit about reining in your kids.

"But if the custodian is your friend, you can get away with a lot of program ideas. You've got someone on your side," says Darrell.

And then there's the Big Save. You don't get them often, but without a friendly custodian you'll never get one at all.

For Darrell, that moment came the night before the grand opening of a sixty-five-thousand-foot church addition.

"The week before we moved in, the senior pastor held a staff meeting and said, 'We've been entrusted with this beautiful building. *Nothing* will happen to it.'

"And I thought, 'I'm dead. I'm the junior high pastor and there's *no way* I can keep a building perfect. We're going to break a window, stain a carpet, or something.'"

The next Saturday, at 8:00pm, Darrell was moving the junior high stuff into the new room. As he pushed a cart loaded with PA equipment down a hall, the cart got away from him.

"The cart hit the corner of a wall opposite the main elevator doors and took a six-inch piece out of the drywall. No way could it escape attention," says Darrell.

So he called the custodians.

"My buddy Herb was in.'I'll bring up some spackle and paint,' he said.'I know where the paint is that they used on this building. Be right there.'"

Darrell spent the next hour spackling and painting. The next day, no one noticed a thing.

As far as Darrell knows, they *still* don't know.

How do you treat other staff members at your church? The senior pastor? secretary? custodian? and, if you're very fortunate, your intern or assistant?

Jot a quick note of appreciation to some other staffers today.

Tape a chocolate bar to the one you give the custodian.

24. THE YOUTH PASTOR AND THE THREE BEARS

Les Parrott

It was Les' first month on the job at a large church in Southern California.

"The room where we met in the church was called the upper room. I took it upon myself to redecorate the whole room during the week. Kids left a familiar room one Sunday; when they came back the next week, the room was totally different."

To say the kids were unimpressed is something of an understatement.

When kids came through the door, they looked stunned. "They asked 'What happened to our home? Who's *been* here?'"

"*That* was a mistake," said Les, who quickly pulled together a committee of kids to take another run at redecorating the room.

Les learned that "running a youth group isn't a dictatorship. Effective leadership in a youth group means inclusion."

How are decisions made in your group? What would happen if you made a change? In your ministry, is the process as important as the result?

25. COMMANDOS FOR CHRIST

Dan Gilliam

It's the sort of youth event that almost requires theme music.

During his youth ministry in Cincinnati, Dan Gilliam's group formed a secret service team he dubbed Commandos for Christ. Their goal was to help people in need without revealing their identity.

"The secrecy made it fun," remembers Dan. "Whenever we called a Commandos meeting, I wouldn't announce what our mission would be. Kids just knew to show up at midnight wearing dark clothes and bearing a bag of food."

Because kids were sworn to secrecy (so their reward would be in heaven, not on earth), no one could talk about missions outside the group. Anyone who wanted to know what was up had to show up for the next mission.

One night Dan loaded fifteen kids, Bibles, and bags of groceries into a black van with tinted windows. Off they drove into one of Cincinnati's high-crime districts.

They decided to look for families sitting in the cool night air on well-lit porches. The plan: Pull up in the van, pile out, offer gifts of Bibles and groceries, share a testimony, sing a song, and then disappear into the night.

"As I remember," says Dan, "we made five stops in all, each more effective than the last. Kids loosened up, realizing we were trusting God to make us successful."

Everything went well until the fifth stop when Dan's band of dark-clad suburban kids, bubbling with enthusiasm, piled out of the van and noticed a gang of twenty or thirty young men walking toward them. These young men were wearing leather. They were *not* smiling.

Says Dan, "None of us moved or said a word; we were frozen by the gravity of our situation. To our amazement, none but the very last gang member looked our way as they passed. His glance was as expressionless as if he were looking down an empty street.

"We left—quickly—and the ride home was glorious."

It was a midnight mission so secret even *parents* didn't know where their kids were heading…in a dangerous part of town…for teenagers dressed in dark clothes. Do you see any problem here?

Absolutely. Yet Dan saw tremendous growth in kids when he put them in situations in which they had to rely on God as they served others.

You don't have to endanger your kids' lives to accomplish this growth. Take them to a workcamp (call Group at 1-800-635-0404 for information). Encourage them to work with young kids. Take them to a nursing home.

Step out of your own comfort zone too. What are *you* doing to serve others that's stretching *your* faith? Have you grown too comfortable in your ministry, your situation, your life?

26. WHERE THERE'S SMOKE...
Jeff Baxter

Jeff Baxter believed in giving kids responsibility, so, in his first church ministry, he broke his ministry into teams that teenagers could lead and serve on.

"Some guys wanted to be on the sports ministry team," remembers Jeff. "They went into where we store our sports stuff, and right above it was an attic where we stored church stuff."

Before long Jeff's enterprising leaders had hauled in a ladder, climbed up to the attic, and established an "office." The office was lit by candles, which is hardly the safest lighting solution in a cramped, enclosed attic.

When Jeff discovered the fire hazard (which was easy; the guys gave tours of their new executive suite to everyone, including their parents), he thought he should evict the guys immediately.

"But when I confronted them, I did it backwards," says Jeff. "I should have confronted *them* first. Instead, I went to their moms and dads."

Going straight to the kids' authority figures wasn't a great relationship-builder. Were he to have the chance to do it again, he'd still pull in the parents, but *not* until he'd talked with the kids.

What's your plan for handling conflict and discipline? Have you thought it through ahead of time so you won't have to make a snap decision?

OUT ON A LIMB
Larry Lindquist

Imagine a warm summer day and an invitation from a youth group guy to head down to the river swimming hole.

Add to the picture the possibility that maybe—just *maybe*—you've recently passed some point of no return and can now no longer keep up with the kids.

This realization dawned on Larry Lindquist the moment his swimming companion showed him a "secret" place where a massive tree bent over a river. From one of the largest branches, hung a large rope. Someone had lopped off the top of a dead branch thirty feet up the tree to make a small platform.

The student from Larry's group quickly scrambled up the tree and leaped into space to grab hold of the rope. He then swung out over the river where he let go with a whoop and landed with a huge splash.

"He popped out of the water screaming, 'Your turn!'" remembers Larry.

"It was at this point that I realized that there is a distinction between 'stupid' and 'cool,'" says Larry, who began to carefully climb the dead tree. He balanced on the tiny platform and, with a heartfelt prayer, jumped for the rope.

> *"When I was a child, I talked like a child, I thought like a child, I reasoned like a child. When I became a man, I put childish ways behind me"*
>
> 1 Corinthians 13:11.

He made it.

He didn't break any bones, he didn't miss the rope, and he didn't swan dive into the bushes instead of the water.

But the experience brought a revelation: "You don't *have* to act like a kid to win the heart of a kid. I'm convinced that, if I'd have just stood there and 'spotted' for that kid as he continued to swing (which is what I did the remainder of the day), our relationship would be no different.

"As you grow older in your ministry with youth, learn from my stupidity. There will come a day when a kid will challenge you to do something you know is too risky for you or beyond your ability. That day may not be here yet, but it *will* come. Just smile, say 'no chance,' and be overwhelmed when your kids succeed."

News flash: You're not seventeen anymore.

In the same way you don't expect your body to handle the punishment you could shrug off when you were younger, your kids don't expect you to take it. If you're still trying to keep up with your kids, what are you trying to prove? and to whom?

27. NERD NIGHT
John Cutshall

It was a classic 80s theme: Nerd Night.

"Kids raided their parents' closets, we played Lawrence Welk music, and the place was packed with pocket protectors, high-water pants, and taped glasses," remembers John Cutshall, who organized the event. "It was perfect. We warned kids that this *wouldn't* be the night to bring friends they wanted to impress."

After playing "nerd games," John loaded kids into the church van and hauled them to a local mall. The trip to the mall wasn't part of the advertised program, and the kids were stunned to learn that he expected them to walk through the mall and out the far door where the van would be waiting for them.

"I was the last one through the mall," says John. "The moment I hopped in the van, there was total silence. The kids had been talking, but, when I showed up, it was total silence."

Says John, "The kids were *hot*. They *hated* walking through the mall dressed like nerds. I'd wanted to make this a great object lesson about the importance of what's inside versus what's outside, but I lost their trust when I made them look stupid."

Do your kids trust that you'll never embarrass them, no matter how good the reason? What evidence have you given them that you're trustworthy?

Hint: If you're not sure how to answer this question, ask your kids for input.

28. ZAP!
Keith Olson

A youth ministry tool that was big in some of Southern California's Campus Life clubs back in the late 60s was the "hot seat."

The hot seat was a metal stool connected to a car battery or other power source. Pushing a button would complete the circuit, and whoever was sitting on the stool would get a shot of electricity that launched him or her off the seat.

Believe it or not, the hot seat wasn't considered a torture device or just cause for calling a child-abuse hotline. It was a ministry tool…sort of.

"I built my own hot seat for my work at a church in Southern California," remembers Keith Olson. "It went over just fine."

Then Keith moved to Tucson, Arizona. "In my mind I thought, 'This will be great. Nobody knows anything about hot seats here.' "

So Keith got busy constructing a new hot seat. "I geared it up to get a good three-quarter-inch arc. I started using it, and kids were saying, 'There's no *way* I'm going to do that!' It didn't go at all.

"The pastor saw the order for the materials and said, 'What are you *doing?*' "

Keith pulled the pastor in for a demonstration and immediately ran into technical difficulties.

"I had the hardest time adjusting it," he remembers. "I shocked my butt so many times that I broke out in a cold sweat as I sat on the stool, ready to punch the button."

The pastor understood the concept but was uncomfortable with it.

"He was concerned about injuring kids," says Keith. "And he was concerned about liability issues, which he should have been and which I hadn't even thought about."

The Tucson hot seat was mothballed immediately. "It was an absolute, flaming bomb," says Keith.

"This was an idea of mine," confesses Keith. "I didn't check with the kids or even another church staff member. I was young, brazen, and arrogant enough that I knew I had a great idea. But it wasn't that good."

You've got great ideas too. In five years, you'll think about some of them and shake your head. Some really *are* great ideas.

But you may not understand the culture, the timing, or the politics. You need honest, open input from others to turn a great idea into a workable one.

How open are you to letting your great ideas be modified by others?

SHORT SCREW-UP

Sex With Pastor

Every year Joani Schultz teamed up with her pastor to develop and lead a sexuality course for the junior highers.

"We met to talk once a week to develop the course," remembers Joani. "It wasn't until about a month or so later that I looked back in my calendar and saw there were certain afternoons where I'd written 'Sex with Pastor.'

"I erased *fast*."

29.BANNED
Lyman Coleman

In the early 60s, Lyman Coleman co-opted popular culture and taught youth groups how to set up coffeehouses in basements and storefronts. "Back then, coffeehouses were where kids talked and expressed themselves through poetry," Lyman remembers.

With rock music came a transformation. Coffeehouses weren't about expression any longer; they'd become entertainment venues.

So in the mid-60s, Lyman moved on to organizing "happenings."

"You'd take a pile of junk and create various expressions of something," he says. "Then you put together an art show and let people come to see it."

The idea caught on. Then, in 1965, Lyman received a phone call.

"The Mennonite church invited me to work with them to prepare for a national youth convention in Estes Park, Colorado," says Lyman.

The Mennonites wanted Lyman to develop a program that turned a study of the book of Acts into more than a stale Bible study. So Lyman drew on his experience in blending art, music, discussion, and theology to write a book about how to integrate self-expression with spiritual growth.

To help the Mennonite youth groups pull off the activities, Lyman included photos of kids actually doing them. He shot the photos at a Baptist camp and a Mennonite high school, so he figured they were safe to use.

Wrong.

"The director of the Mennonite Publishing House called the night before the book was printed," remembers Lyman. "He said, 'Someone has seen the plates, and we can't publish the book. There are girls in the photographs without prayer hats on. We painted the legs of girls who were wearing shorts, but we can't put prayer hats on the girls. We still want to use the book, but we've got to make some changes.'"

It was too late for massive revisions, so Lyman suggested that the publisher simply change the name of the book to *Acts Alive* to indicate a change in emphasis. And a new name was created under which to publish it. *Acts Alive* became a groundbreaking youth ministry bestseller.

"When the book was printed and sent to the Mennonite churches, three bishops banned it," says Lyman. "That's how the book became a bestseller: As soon as they banned it, every church in America wanted it."

A "mistake" nearly derailed Lyman's youth ministry. A publisher's last-minute panic about prayer hats launched both the Serendipity House publishing company and a national movement to help kids experience and express their faith.

What are "mistakes" in your ministry that have proven to be opportunities for God to work? What does that tell you about God? About yourself?

ALL-STAR ADVICE

Ministry and Marriage

Les Parrott has had ample opportunity to observe ministry marriages as he's led marriage workshops.

His advice to youth workers who are, or will be, married: "Learn to balance your marriage and ministry. Don't let the ministry swallow up your whole marriage to the extent that you don't have a marriage outside the ministry realm.

"Let your spouse have a say about joining you on an overnight trip or any other programs. Don't make assumptions about your spouse's participation."

Churches are often all too happy to get "two for the price of one." The time to be clear that that's not the case is up front, not after you've established unhealthy patterns.

30. WHAT THE...?

Bryan Belknap

When Bryan Belknap worked in college ministry, he had a bad habit: He cussed. He didn't do it all the time, and he didn't do it in front of students. When Bryan was surprised or startled, though, inappropriate language sometimes burst out.

Maybe it was just a bad habit, or maybe it was the influence of the culture in which he was raised. Whatever the reason, Bryan wasn't proud of his vocabulary, and God was dealing with him about the problem.

Then something happened that pushed the issue from back-burner simmer to full front-burner boil.

"We were on a church ski trip, and I nearly got in a wreck," says Bryan. "I was driving the van, and, when I pulled out to pass someone, there was an eighteen-wheeler coming right at us. I swerved back in time, but I said something without thinking. There was absolute silence in the van.

"Then I acknowledged my sin to you and did not cover up my iniquity. I said, 'I will confess my transgressions to the Lord'—and you forgave the guilt of my sin"

Psalm 32:5.

I don't know if kids were more shocked because of what I said or because we nearly died."

"I said, 'Sorry. I'm so sorry.' "

What might have been a career-ending mistake didn't alienate the kids or disrupt his ministry. Why? Kids already knew Bryan had a problem with language. While preaching a sermon about what people dealt with in their Christian lives, he'd confessed he sometimes struggled with his language.

"I was honest about my shortcomings," says Bryan. "I presented myself to kids as a work in progress, just like them."

Maybe it's your bad language, a lack of compassion, a habit, or cynicism. Whatever it is, *something* in your life makes you less than perfect.

Sooner or later, it will come out. If you've let your kids believe you're a perfect, ideal believer, their disappointment will be staggering.

Even worse: If nobody sees through your façade, your perfectionism may alienate you from your kids.

Be human. Be a passionate believer. Be both.

31. QUIET AS A CHURCH ELEPHANT
Dan Slatter

After becoming a Christian at age sixteen, Dan Slatter began attending an Anglican church in England. "They didn't know what to do with me because I was still something of a terror," Dan remembers. "Their solution was to put me in charge of one of the youth groups. I'd been a Christian about five minutes."

To help move the youth group from "babysitting" to something deeper, Dan decided to do a lock-in with the kids.

"Kids who turned up were like myself: totally unchurched," says Dan. "When they walked into a church building, they didn't quiet down, and they respected it about as much as they respected their school. They slammed doors and kicked holes in walls when nobody was looking."

About thirty twelve- and thirteen-year-old kids came to the lock-in. Only three were Christians.

"It was absolute chaos," says Dan. "We were in an old church hall, and it was such good fun. But it was complete pandemonium; it was a riot."

"My brothers, as believers in our glorious Lord Jesus Christ, don't show favoritism"

James 2:1.

Dan knew things had tipped over the edge when the church custodian, who lived in a flat above the hall, came down the stairs screaming that he'd just called the police. "He thought there were people being beaten up and attacked."

After quieting the kids down, Dan had them sit in a circle and asked, "If you could ask God to change one thing in your life, what would it be?"

He was stunned at the response. "These hardened kids opened up about things they hadn't told anyone. They were crying and talking about their home lives. It was fantastic."

Yet the week after the lock-in, when the same kids turned up again, "the place got absolutely trashed. Mirrors were broken in the toilets, and a light was smashed off the ceiling," says Dan. "The vicar told me I was banned from youth work and the kids weren't allowed back in the church. I managed to talk him into letting me stay if they put another adult in there with me.

"But the kids stayed banned."

Dan will tell you that his lack of experience as a youth leader is one reason his kids got out of hand. And he understands the vicar's hesitation to pay for repairs after every youth meeting.

What do you do with kids who simply don't respect God or your church building? Are they welcome or not?

How open are you—and your ministry—to kids who are different from you?

32. I DUNNO. WHAT DO YOU WANT TO DO?
Tim Smith

At Tim Smith's first youth ministry, he ministered to a grand total of seven kids. "I felt small, insignificant, and embarrassed," he recalls, remembering the times his one-car youth group

> *"I thank my God every time I remember you. In all my prayers for all of you, I always pray with joy because of your partnership in the gospel from the first day until now, being confident of this, that he who began a good work in you will carry it on to completion until the day of Christ Jesus"*
>
> Philippians 1:3-6.

pulled into a parking lot where bus-size youth groups were gathering for an event.

"Because I was more concerned about being liked than being a leader, I seldom challenged my students to serve or lead. I challenged them to study the Bible, to pray, and to attend youth group, but I hadn't yet learned the value of *praxis,* or the art of practicing what you've learned."

It took a hard question from one of the kids to move Tim ahead.

"Robert was the intellectual in the group," says Tim. "He asked, 'How long do you think it takes before we're ready to do something about what you've been teaching?'

"'A little longer?' I sheepishly responded."

So Tim called a leadership meeting, and six of his seven kids showed up. Tim asked what they thought of his easing up on the lecturing and letting them talk more. They agreed enthusiastically, then they carried it a step further.

Not only would they get with that program, they'd help make it happen by jumping in to find a meeting room, coordinating with an area Campus Life club, and even doing service projects.

"I sat there dumbfounded," says Tim. "There was more energy and motivation in that room during that one meeting than had been there in the previous six months. I realized then that I'd failed to understand that most teenagers want to be challenged to lead or serve. All we need to do is offer them choices."

"When I think of it, I may have done more harm than good in terms of the kids' spiritual journey," says Tim of his first youth group. "They learned from me, their youth pastor, that Christianity is something you know not something you do."

What's your youth group learning from watching you? Is your leadership style an empowering one that helps kids do something with what they know? Have you asked them lately what they'd like to do?

Remember: It's their youth group. And God leads kids, too.

33. SMOKEY AND THE SHOTGUN
Dan Gilliam

While en route to a mountaintop retreat in Tennessee, Dan Gilliam's Ohio youth group noticed that fireworks, which were illegal in Ohio, were readily available in Tennessee.

So the youth group stopped to load up.

"The next logical step was to locate a remote area to shoot them off," explains Dan, who soon spied a suitable wooded area.

"We divided up into teams, and the bottle-rocket-smoke-bomb battle was on," says Dan.

A rule was quickly established: Whenever a brush fire started, time out was called so everyone could help stomp the fire out. Then the battle resumed.

"After launching missiles and putting out fires for half an hour, someone yelled for cease fire. I assumed we had another blaze to extinguish.

"Instead, there were two park rangers with shotguns on their shoulders, chewing tobacco and looking for whoever was in charge of the fight."

To Dan's relief, the rangers simply stopped the war by explaining what should have been obvious: Because of a drought, the woods were extremely dry. No charges were filed, and no one was arrested.

We've all been there. Because we want kids to have a good time and hate being spoilsports, we OK things we could *never* explain at a board meeting. Which are you in your youth group: a buddy or a leader?

34. THE ONE AND ONLY
Rollie Martinson

When Rollie Martinson began his first yearlong ministry internship, his supervisor challenged him to get a youth ministry started in that congregation.

"I did it," says Rollie. "Even though I had some adults with me, so much of what I did focused on me as a committed Christian who was young, enthusiastic, and energetic."

There was one major high school and one junior high school, and Rollie worked hard to form relationships with the kids. It worked…sort of.

"In one year, we created an active, large youth ministry." That was the good news.

The bad news was that Rollie had committed two cardinal youth ministry sins. The first was that he hadn't built on a firm foundation. "The ministry was essentially focused around me, not Jesus Christ," remembers Rollie.

Rollie's second mistake was playing Lone Ranger to get the ministry up and running. "It wasn't built on the infrastructure of Christ's body, so my leaving resulted in a mess for the person who came after me."

Still, there was an active youth ministry when he left and none when he came. So, to Rollie, it looked like a success, a success he repeated almost immediately.

"I went from that internship to a second parish while I spent another year finishing my seminary training," he says.

Rollie didn't know the full extent of the damage he'd done until five years later when he attended a conference and met the person who followed him in that second church. "When that person met me, the first words out of his mouth were, 'I hate you. I had to follow what you'd done developing a ministry that was dependent on you and your style.'

"He was absolutely right. Those two classic mistakes nearly fried me while, at the same time, they nearly crippled the long-term, ongoing ministries of those two congregations."

Says Rollie, "The quick fix many congregations take is to bring in a Lone Ranger who can single-handedly step out and lead. People think they can bring in an instant youth ministry by bringing in the right leader.

"But good youth ministries are never bought and never instantly created.

"They're always developed, custom designed, and organically grown in the soil of that particular context in a period of five to seven years."

The question: What would happen to your ministry if you were to die tomorrow? or go elsewhere?

Have you taken time to develop leadership in others who would sustain the ministry? Are others prepared to carry on without you?

35. TWELVE O'CLOCK AND ALL IS WELL

Lynn Ziegenfuss

It was New Years Eve, 1976.

On a night most people were out celebrating, Lynn Ziegenfuss found herself alone, wrestling with God.

"I'd come home from a camp we'd done with kids," remembers Lynn. "It was about 9:00 p.m., and my friends were going out to have fun."

But Lynn felt troubled, so she stayed behind. And that night, from about 10:30 to 12:30, she dealt with issues that had been building during her first six months in full-time ministry.

"Truly it was about surrendering the ministry to God and understanding that this was where he was going to mold my character. Anything he allowed to happen was going to be his work, and I had the privilege of being the tool."

Lynn now realizes that her experience that New Year's Eve shouldn't have come as a surprise.

Six months before, at Youth for Christ's national training school, YFC president Jay Kesler had looked into the eyes of Lynn's enthusiastic class of new recruits. "He told us he hoped that, within the next year, we'd all find ourselves prostrate on the floor, crying out to God for his help."

"You're excited and go into ministry with all these expectations, and it's always harder than you thought," says Lynn.

"One of the reasons it's that way is the expectation that you're going to do this great ministry. In fact the first year is more about discovering your own gifts, your limits, and how to master your schedule.

"Through college your schedule is set for you by classes or maybe a job. Ministry means that, in many ways, you're the master of your time. You have to learn to manage your life. It's very easy to run ahead of God and not lean into him. Instead you try to prove yourself."

Lynn challenges new YFC recruits to stay in ministry three years before they allow themselves to question whether they should quit. "Your third year is where you experience the fruit," says Lynn. "When people make a decision to leave after a year, they're usually making a bad decision. What young people don't understand is that it takes three years to build a ministry."

Have you made at least a three-year commitment to ministry? Why, or why not?

ALL-STAR ADVICE

An Impossible Situation

Here's an impossible situation for you.

When Dwight Robertson was barely eighteen, a church with nearly one thousand members invited him to become a youth leader.

"I said no three or four times," remembers Dwight. "Finally the associate youth pastor called and said, 'I'm not sure why you keep saying no. You and I both know God's told you to do this. What's your problem?'

"I said, 'That's simple: I'm younger than some of the kids in the youth group. I have no experience. I wouldn't know where to begin.'"

Yet, in spite of those shortcomings, Dwight signed on.

And in spite of the odds, Dwight succeeded beyond all expectations. Here's how:

He prayed. "I cried out to God that I just couldn't do it," remembers Dwight. "I prayed my way through. I had such a smooth experience that the poor guys who came after me kept being compared to the successes that God gave me."

He didn't try to do it alone. Dwight pulled together a group of "highly dedicated, spiritually committed college students" who became small-group leaders in his high school ministry. "Those folks were instruments in the hands of God."

He didn't try to import someone else's success. "I drew on my own personal journey instead of trying to duplicate things I'd seen other places," he says. It's tempting to assume that if something works at Willow Creek, Saddleback, or down the street, it'll work with your kids, but that's not necessarily so.

Dwight stressed the spiritual disciplines. He stressed quiet times, worship, and prayer. "I think most young people are overly entertained and underchallenged spiritually," says Dwight. His kids rose to the level of the spiritual challenge put before them.

36. ANOTHER REASON YOU SHOULD ALWAYS TAKE GOOD CARE OF YOUR SENIOR PASTOR

Les Christie

During a youth group all-nighter, Les Christie organized a Polaroid camera scavenger hunt.

Each car-load of adults and kids got a Polaroid camera and a list of pictures to take. The lists of pictures required situations such as being in a police car and being stuffed into a laundromat clothes dryer. You know, *fun* stuff.

"I had our guest speaker and four high school kids in my car," says Les. "It was 1 a.m., and we'd just finished taking a picture of our group crammed into one of the old-fashioned, enclosed telephone booths.

"We were in a K-Mart parking lot to get a picture of the kids on a horsey ride when two police cars with flashing lights arrived.

"The police asked who was in charge. When I stepped forward, they leaned me against a police car and frisked me. The kids and our guest speaker were lined up against a wall.

"Three *more* police cars arrived from neighboring districts. Now I'm worried, and I'm explaining to an officer who we are and what we're doing."

The officer told Les that a neighbor near the telephone booth had seen a flash and phoned in to report that the kids had blown up the booth.

> "I thank my God every time I remember you"
>
> Philippians 1:3.

Les knew it had simply been the camera flash, but the week before, someone *had* blown up a telephone booth in the area. The police were taking no chances.

"I told them who I was and what I was doing, and I asked them to call Ben, the senior pastor, to verify my identity. An officer called Ben—remember, it's 1 a.m.—and explained the situation.

"And Ben said, 'I've never heard of the guy' and hung up.

"Things got pretty sticky after that," remembers Les.

He was finally set free when the police drove by the telephone booth and confirmed that it had not, in fact, exploded.

Senior pastors can make or break your youth ministry. Les worked twenty-two years with Ben and values every minute of their time together. "I got him back," says Les, "But that's another story."

How's your relationship with your senior pastor? your church board?

Do you ever laugh together, share stories, and come through for each other?

Ask God for specific opportunities to get to know the people on your church team. Seek ways to connect with and affirm them. Start this week with the ideas you jot down here:

WHAT WALLET?
Thom Schultz

Thom Schultz's youth group was on a ski trip to the mountains, where they bunked in a church basement.

"One of the kids who came along was a friend of a regular attender and wasn't what you'd call a goody-goody church kid," remembers Thom. Because Thom wanted his group to reach out and include others, the young man was readily accepted.

Then a wallet disappeared. During the weekend, one of the kids, who happened to be the son of a church leader, announced that his wallet had been stolen. In front of the entire group, he said he was sure he knew who'd taken it—the newcomer.

"The kids got upset and started accusing each other," says Thom. "So we looked through everything. We couldn't find the wallet. I pulled the kids together and asked if they'd seen it, assuring them that, if anyone *had* happened to pick it up by mistake, it could be returned anonymously."

But no one stepped forward. The group that drove down the mountain was far less united than the group that had driven up it.

"On the way home, retracing our journey, we stopped at the same gas station we'd stopped at on our way to the retreat," says Thom. "The first thing the kid who'd lost his wallet did was run into the restroom to look around. Then he asked the gas station attendants if they'd seen his wallet.

> *"A patient man has great understanding, but a quick-tempered man displays folly"*
>
> Proverbs 14:29.

"I said, 'I thought you lost your wallet at the church.'

"The young man answered that he wasn't sure. The last time he'd *seen* the wallet had been at the gas station."

Thom concluded on the spot that the wallet had probably been left at the gas station. He drove the rest of the way back to the church, and the kids headed home.

"Shortly after the kids got to their homes, I got a call from the church leader," Thom remembers. "He was *livid* about the way I'd handled the situation. He asked me if I'd lined the kids up and searched them.

"I said, 'You mean like a *strip* search?'

" 'Well, if that's what it takes!' he shouted."

Thom explained that the boy wasn't even sure his wallet had been stolen and had admitted as much. But the boy's story had changed, and the father's negative feelings about the incident continued throughout Thom's ministry at the church.

"One of the things I did right was to *not* line up kids and accuse them," says Thom. "Similar things have happened since, and usually whatever was lost turned up later. You've got to deal with the situation delicately.

"But I should have been proactive with that parent. I should have been in contact during the retreat or immediately when we got home, *before* things got blown out of proportion."

Proactive communication means thinking through how a situation *might* be understood, considering how a word or incident *might* be interpreted, and how a situation *might* play for those who weren't there to witness it.

What are you doing to proactively communicate with parents? What else could you do?

Are you slow to accuse or condemn?

37. FIRST THINGS FIRST
Dan Jessup

While attending seminary at Princeton, Dan Jessup worked with a New Jersey youth group. "I was writing the best youth studies I'd ever written," says Dan. "I was loading them up with Greek and Hebrew, really getting in and getting deep."

And did his grateful youth group hang on his every word?

Not exactly.

"The kids blew it off. They were totally not interested, not growing in their faith," remembers Dan. "After about three months, I was angry. Then I realized the kids were just reflecting my life. I was so wrapped up in my studies that I'd walked away from serving Christ. Not that I wasn't a Christian—I was—but I wasn't *loving* the kids.

"I was teaching them the Bible, but they were learning my life."

Dan realized that an effective ministry required that he be "a little less about study and a little more about loving kids."

Do your kids know you love them? For that matter—*do* you love them? Have they invited you to speak into their lives? Why, or why not?

38. HOW NOT TO DO CONFLICT RESOLUTION
Monty Hipp

It happens.

In a youth group Monty Hipp was leading, a guy and girl got sexually involved, and the girl became pregnant.

Monty decided to help the kids' fathers come to an understanding.

"I put the two dads in the same room, thinking we'd be the body of Christ and work things out.

"It got worked out all right," says Monty. "It got worked *over*. I had to try to pull them apart. They were *livid* with each other."

> *"Blessed are the peacemakers, for they will be called sons of God"*
> Matthew 5:9.

Conflicts will arise in your youth group, and working for resolution is a great idea. But you need to be wise in how you go about it.

Where's there conflict in your group now? In what ways could you be a wise peacemaker?

39. THE DARKEST HOUR
Steve Munds

It's every youth worker's nightmare…and it happened to Steve Munds.

"I lost a kid," says Steve quietly. "I took ninety-nine kids to a Florida youth conference and brought back ninety-eight. One of the girls was hit by a car while crossing the road. She died instantly."

Kids were not supposed to cross the street outside their hotel without an adult present. They used a buddy system. The night the young woman was killed, she obeyed all the rules.

Yet it still happened. Steve felt the full weight of the loss.

"I sat in the hospital at 2:00 a.m. and told God, 'Lord, I quit. I can't handle this. It's over. You entrusted these kids to me, I entrusted them to you, and I lose a kid. This isn't for me.'"

Describing the dark hours in the hospital, Steve says, "I was feeling sorry for myself, though I didn't realize it.

"The Lord began dealing with me. He said, 'You need to get back to your youth group. The ninety-eight still sitting there need a word from you.'

"I went to a Scripture in Romans, which says whether we live or whether we die, we're the Lord's."

That passage encouraged Steve, though he still intended to leave the ministry. He headed back to the hotel where the rest of his kids waited in stunned silence.

As Steve walked into the hotel, the manager asked if he was Steve Munds. A long distance call waited for him: It was from the girl's father.

Steve will never forget the first words the father said. "Steve," came the steady voice of a father who had just lost his daughter, "I sent my kid to Florida with you so she would find Jesus. And you know what? She did."

Emotion still chokes Steve's voice as he talks about the trip home. "God's strength, mercy, and grace helped us through it. When we got back to the church, the first people who greeted us in the parking lot were the girl's parents. They embraced me and said, 'Steve, we don't hold you responsible.'"

Did Steve make a mistake? Yes…but a very human one.

"My first reaction was to blame God. My second reaction was to blame me. I kept thinking, 'God, if I can't trust you to take care of the kids and I can't trust myself, what am I doing in this job?'"

Steve's mistake was in not simply trusting God to do his will through the tragedy. "In every death, something gets established," says Steve. He says the life—and the death—of the young woman he took to Florida continues to prompt growth in countless lives.

Tragedy can hit any ministry. In your group, it may be a car wreck, an unwanted pregnancy, the death of a youngster en route to a concert.

How will you respond? You'll be tempted to quit, but will you?

ALL-STAR ADVICE

Avoiding Ministry-Ending Mistakes

You're going to do a certain number of truly dumb things because you're human. Welcome to Humility 101.

But you can avoid many of the ministry-ending mistakes that thin the ranks of youth ministry by considering these nuggets of advice from Bob Laurent.

Don't rely on people for your self-worth. "Don't expect people to stroke your ego or give you confidence," says Bob. "You can get in lots of trouble when you're looking for encouragement and it doesn't come. And it may *not* come for a long time. The input you get may be more negative than positive for awhile."

One possible outcome of falling into this trap is a very real risk of sexual immorality.

"We lose youth workers to sexual immorality in part because, when they don't get strokes from the senior pastor or encouragement from parents and other church staff, they look for good feelings where they can find them."

Be an encourager. "Don't be a false flatterer," says Bob, "Instead be someone who finds something good in any situation and every person." This practiced trait will not only keep you positive but naturally draw you to other encouragers.

Expect to suffer. Bob considers 1 Peter 4:1 an important verse for youth workers to embrace. Says Bob, "If you don't have a mind to suffer, *every* parent is going to give you trouble. *Every* student is going to be a rascal. But if you have a mind to suffer, then you won't have to be broken—the way most of us are."

And yet youth ministry is a wonderful opportunity for joy and seeing lives change. "As a youth worker, you're continually with people who are still pliable and open enough to make significant life changes," says Bob. "There's a lot of joy there."

Hey, it's ministry. It's *supposed* to stretch and challenge you.

When hard times come, don't let them make you bitter. "Youth ministers become dysfunctional through bitterness. Bitterness affects your kids and your relationships with friends and family. Don't fall prey to bitterness," cautions Bob. A passage to meditate on is Hebrews 12:15.

Be *realistically* idealistic. "Every youth minister is idealistic," says Bob. "But there's a difference between having unrealistic expectations and being truly idealistic and optimistic. *Be* idealistic and optimistic, but don't set unrealistic goals."

Even in times of dashed expectations and failure, "Keep your ideals high and hold onto promises God has made to you. Believe that God can produce much fruit," says Bob.

Don't take too much credit for your successes...or too much blame for your failures. "It's ironic, but pretty much the same thing happened to me in both situations," says Bob. "After five hundred teenagers accepted Christ in one night, I became too full of myself, which messed up my relationships with important people. Being too down on myself also messed up my relationships with important people."

Don't forget who powers your ministry and who's molding you.

Seek to be stable. The ability God wants most to see in youth ministers is stability. "They're working with kids who are on an emotional roller coaster. Just to have someone in kids' lives who's stable and levelheaded is a wonderful gift."

Can your kids count on you to be a steady place to rest?

Build God-honoring friendships for love and accountability. "Look for someone who'll tell you the truth about yourself and still love you. Get at least two of these people in your life," says Bob.

"Singer Michael W. Smith told me that the reason he's stayed sexually pure in spite of having everything in the world thrown at him is that he has three pastors who are continually calling and asking about his thought life."

Never view the parents of your teens as the enemy. Friction usually develops, but you need parents to be a major part of your team.

"Some parents won't like you, but you're ministering to parents as much as you are to teens," says Bob. "You need to remember that. You need parents to be your prayer warriors as much as you need the people who pay the ticket and get the pastor to put you in the budget."

Youth ministry is about delegation. "The job of a youth minister is to equip youth and their parents for the work of the ministry. The youth minister isn't supposed to *do* the work of the youth ministry; he or she is there to *train* others."

If you ever want to step back from the crunch of doing everything yourself, you need to train others to do what you do. It's just that simple.

Don't get too busy for the spiritual disciplines. Says Bob, "You can't have successful ministry if you're too busy for the disciplines of fasting, meditating on the Bible, praying, and getting to know God."

Make sure your job description includes time for spiritual formation. An excellent passage for meditation about yourself and your ministry is Psalm 119:165.

40. ROADSIDE FACULTY

Andy Hansen

As dean of a week of camp for two-hundred junior high kids, Andy Hansen had recruited the best staff he could find. "I had more than thirty people," remembers Andy, who was confident they'd have a great experience.

"I arrived with a bus-load of kids from our church. As we rumbled into camp, I noticed there were scads of kids tearing around and a lot of very unhappy parents.

"On the other side of the road were all my faculty members. And they weren't crossing the road."

Andy bounced off the church bus and ran to where his staff people were waiting. "I said, 'What's the deal? Come on! We've got to get the kids into the cabins.'

"I quickly found out I'd forgotten to inform my faculty that they all had to have tuberculosis shots. State law required a tuberculosis shot before you could be a worker on the campground."

A government official had recently inspected the camp, so the camp manager wasn't taking any chances with nonvaccinated faculty. "They couldn't even step on the property without shots," says Andy.

A nurse showed up to administer the vaccine, and Andy remembers how pleased his handpicked faculty were about having to roll up their sleeves for a shot before they could unpack their bags. He also remembers how pleased parents were about waiting for faculty vaccinations before they could leave. The camp manager, too, was annoyed.

"Everyone was pretty excited about me on my first day," says Andy.

OK, so you're not a detail kind of person. That's one reason you're in youth ministry, right?

Sooner or later, you'll overlook a critical detail that derails a project. How will you handle it when it happens? Will you admit your mistakes and move on, or point fingers until you find someone else to blame?

Benefit from Andy's example: Humbly take your lumps and move ahead.

41. THE FIRST— AND LAST— VISIT

Mike Nappa

It was game time, and the gym was packed with junior highers. Perched on a platform fifteen feet above the gym floor where he could keep an eye on the mayhem below, stood Mike Nappa.

"We were playing a version of the game Steal the Bacon," remembers Mike. The game involved placing kids against all four walls and putting a stack of items in the middle of the gym. When Mike gave a signal, kids ran out and tried to grab the items with the highest point value for their team. A traffic cone might be worth twenty-five points, and a Frisbee might be worth fifty points. "The big-ticket item was a rope. It was worth five hundred points," recalls Mike.

"We were about out of time, and I wanted to make sure everyone had played, so I signaled that everyone on all four teams would play the next round. It was absolute bedlam with two hundred and fifty junior high kids grabbing for stuff at the same time," says Mike.

"One little girl—a first time visitor—reached for a Frisbee and got her arms caught in the rope while kids from all four teams were pulling on it."

One of Mike's volunteers was a nurse. After looking at the girl, he told Mike he thought her arms were broken.

"I'd just watched the game, and I was sure nothing happened that could have broken any bones," says Mike. "I told him to put some ice on her arms; she'd be fine."

When the arms continued to swell, the nurse returned. He still thought there were broken bones.

"At this point, I was getting ready to speak to the kids, so I told him, if he thought it was really bad, to keep ice on it and call her parents," says Mike.

The nurse did as Mike suggested, and the girl's parents drove her straight to the hospital where an X-ray confirmed the nurse's diagnosis of two broken arms.

"Fortunately the parents didn't sue us," says Mike, "but they forbid her to ever come back to our church."

Mike didn't earn any points for how he handled this situation, and he doesn't expect any.

"I was careless about the game I conducted and heartless about the consequences of the game," says Mike.

Were he to have the chance to do it over, kids would not be playing that particular game at all. "I'd do a better job of thinking through the safety issues," he says.

How safe are kids in your ministry? physically? emotionally? spiritually?

42. BREAKING AWAY

Darrell Pearson

Back in the early 80s, Darrell Pearson and Jim Hancock were in charge of a week of junior and senior high camp.

"We were going to show the movie *Breaking Away* " remembers Darrell. "We'd ordered the movie months in advance. When it arrived, Jim said, 'It's been awhile since I saw the film. I'm remembering it might be too intense to show to junior highers.' "

When Darrell and Jim previewed the film, they found that, sure enough, it was peppered with bad language and sexually suggestive situations.

What to do? They'd already announced a movie night, and, in those pre-video-rental days, they couldn't just go pick up a different film.

"We told the counselors that we couldn't show the movie, but they said, 'No! We've *got* to have the movie!' " Jim had forgotten that movie night was the counselors' night off. They could simply sit and relax while the movie played.

A compromise was hammered out: Darrell watched the movie again, noting each time an inappropriate word or scene appeared. He figured he'd sit next to the projector and, when something questionable was about to happen, he'd edit it out. Problem solved.

Almost.

"I missed the first ten words to come up by a split second," Darrell remembers. "Someone would swear, and then it'd be totally quiet. I was *emphasizing* the swear words.

"There's one scene in which some high school guys are watching a college coed jog and commenting on her physique. I shut the sound off for the whole scene. Our kids all sat in the silence, in the dark, while on screen these guys are *obviously* talking about the jogger.

"I got to the end of the scene and turned up the sound *just* in time to hear a slang word for a very specific part of her anatomy blasted at full volume."

Do you think you're fast enough to edit a film or video as your kids watch it? You're not, at least not effectively. Your kids are media gurus; they'll fill in the blanks you make even if you delete segments.

Do you take the time to preview video clips and other resources you bring into your youth room? Remember: What you expose kids to comes with your endorsement—even if you didn't intend to give one.

43. THROUGH PARENTS' EYES
Joani Schultz

Joani Schultz remembers a time her youth group was late returning from an event.

"Sitting in the parking lot was a mom who'd always been supportive. But for whatever reason, that night she was furious. I walked up to her car after her son was in it to talk with her. She rolled up the window, and the tires squealed as she sped out of the parking lot.

"There I stood, feeling terrible. I knew I probably should have called to say we'd be late, but those were the days before cell phones.

"The next day I called her up and said, 'I need to talk to you.' I went to her home, and she met me with a big hug. She felt bad, I felt bad, and we sat and talked through it. It felt great to be forgiven.

"Relationships with parents are worth it. Always."

OK, so you were late. It wasn't your fault. You did what you could.

Don't count on parents to understand your good intentions. They only know that you showed up at 1:00 a.m. instead of the promised 11:30 p.m.

How do you view parents in your ministry? Are they your friends or your foes? What have you done to make them your friends?

This week phone the parents of three kids. Thank the parents for letting their kids participate. Ask what suggestions the parents have for improving your youth program—and *listen*.

Busy-ness

Larry Acosta nearly went down the tubes as his ministry grew.

"When I first got started in youth ministry, I was over-programmed. I was so busy trying to take care of details and be at all the meetings that the 'busyness' kept me from cultivating my heart for God.

"We tell kids that there's power in meeting with God, but it's easy for us to get so busy that we fail to do it.

"Our busyness isn't a sign of our success. It's a tool of Satan to keep us from a power-filled Christian experience. I didn't realize that until later."

44. THE YOUTH-O-RAMA

Barry St. Clair

During Barry St. Clair's first few months in youth ministry, he and his wife decided to make a huge splash with a spectacular event for the kids—one that would grab attention and pull in a gazillion visitors.

"We had a 'Teen-O-Rama,'" remembers Barry. (Note to the reader: this *was* the 60s.) The idea was to meet the kids early on a Saturday, ride in a rented bus to a fun event, then do missions projects. We had a full day planned."

Barry didn't skimp on publicity. "We really pushed it hard. The pastor pushed it from the pulpit, I talked with the kids about it on numerous occasions, and we talked with the parents," he says.

So with high hopes and a full agenda, Barry and his wife showed up at 8:00 a.m. on the designated Saturday.

Waiting for them was a rented bus, a bored driver, and precisely no kids.

"Even the chaperones didn't show up," says Barry, who was eventually joined by two teenagers.

"It was horrible. Now I'd just tell the two kids to go on home, but what we did back then was push ahead. We spent the entire day doing what we'd planned, and it was awful."

Barry later realized he was guilty of several significant sins.

"We'd done the program without a process of involving the kids. We were new and didn't have relationships with the kids, so they didn't trust us. And parents didn't know if they could trust us with their kids."

"Plus," adds Barry with twenty-twenty hindsight, "We had a *horrible* name for the event."

As bad as the day was—and Barry confirms it was a long, discouraging day—there was a payoff in Barry's ministry.

"This was the start of my understanding that it's not the event but the *process* that makes the difference. The activities we do in youth group are pretty much irrelevant compared to the relationships we have with kids and our involvement in their lives.

"We'd come in from the outside and decided what the kids needed. And they obviously *didn't* need it, because they didn't show up."

Relationships and events: If you had to choose just one as a focus, which would you pick?

The fact is that you *do* have to select a primary focus for your ministry, because multiple approaches compete with each other. It's tough to plan mega-events and still have time to go hang around with kids at lunchtime.

How's your relationship with your kids? What could you do to improve it this week? Write one specific thing you'll do below:

_____

_____

_____

ALL-STAR ADVICE

First, De-Stress. Then *Discuss.*

Uh-oh. When the kids' water balloon fight escalated, the Senior Saints' Petunia Praise Garden got stomped flat. Now there are three angry grandmas lined up outside your office, and one of them is carrying pruning scissors.

Before opening your door, take thirty seconds to de-stress.

1. Take three deep, slow breaths.

2. Relax your muscles. Open and close your fists a few times, let your shoulders drop, and do a few head rolls.

3. Stretch once to ease the tension building in your back.

4. Rank how deep a hole you're in on a scale of one to ten and respond appropriately. Don't stress at level ten (hyperventilating, frantic resume revising, reciting Psalm 23 aloud) if it's a level-three problem.

Decide to listen and to *communicate* that you're listening. Don't compound your problems by coming off as a know-it-all or as indifferent. Be ready to empathize and restate the concerns of those confronting you.

You can always tell the youth group that replanting those petunias is a service project.

ALL-STAR ADVICE

How to Team Up With Your Senior Pastor

They're big. They're bad. They're overpaid and don't have to deal with lock-ins.

They're senior pastors.

Talking with groups of youth workers might give you the sense that senior pastors are the enemy. Overall that's not the case.

"It's a myth," says Dr. Keith Olson. "It's a classic example of a generation gap thing. By and large, most senior pastors I interact with are very interested in giving their youth ministers as much latitude as they can to bring fresh, new energy to the ministry."

Make no mistake: Your senior pastor can give your ministry a tremendous boost. Your senior pastor can also torpedo you in a heartbeat. If you get your relationship with that staff member in order, you'll avoid huge headaches.

"Remember: Your senior pastor may save your bacon," says John Cutshall. "You'd better be on good terms."

Here are five ways to be sure you and your senior pastor are on the same page.

Be connected.

Go to lunch now and then. Ask advice. Pray together. Don't let the time you screw up be the first time you've had a heart-to-heart talk. Let your senior pastor be a resource to you and your ministry.

Even if your senior pastor doesn't value youth ministry and has seen ten youth pastors come and go, make the effort. Your kids are watching, and your attitude is obvious.

Respect your senior pastor.

Speak highly of your senior pastor to your kids and their families. And, if you don't want the senior pastor second-guessing your decisions, don't second-guess his or hers.

Says Dan Jessup, "The senior pastor is in charge. You may think, 'I'm the one who understands the kids and knows what to do, and you may be right. But the senior pastor is still the person God put in your life as an authority. So be 'leadable.'"

Keep your senior pastor posted.

When you make a mistake, it won't necessarily be you who gets the midnight call. Brief your senior pastor about upcoming plans, current successes and failures, and anything that you think will sound better coming from you than in a late-night phone call from an irate parent. If anything particularly ticklish arises, bring your senior pastor into the loop immediately.

Keep backstage issues backstage.

You're going to have disagreements with your senior pastor, and the place to handle them is behind closed doors. If you need to vent your feelings, do so with your spouse, fellow youth workers, or a trusted friend—but not with your kids or others in the church. Be professional.

Learn from your senior pastor.

If your senior pastor has worked with kids, take advantage of that experience.

Dan Slatter, who leads the youth portion of England's Revelation Church, says, "Our church was started as a youth church seventeen years ago. Roger, who led it all, made a lot of those first mistakes. So now there's someone standing around who can say, 'Dan, I've been there and done that, and here's what normally happens. Maybe this isn't such a great idea, but what about something else?'"

If you've got a senior pastor in your life who knows how to be encouraging, take advantage of it. It's a rare gift.

45. THE CANDLE
Bob Laurent

When Bob Laurent started in youth ministry, he spent nights working on music and days working on his Master of Divinity degree. It was a challenging schedule that soon got worse.

"We hooked up with the Billy Graham Evangelistic Association," Bob remembers, "and went around doing high school assemblies for them."

Bob's band played at *lots* of high school assemblies. The band performed at some eight hundred public school assemblies in a remarkably short time. Then performances for Campus Crusade and other organizations were added to the load.

"We started at 7:00 a.m. and went until 2:00 a.m. every day. There were people who wanted us in the morning and people who wanted us at night. That's what youth ministry will do to you," says Bob.

The time on the road and the constant pressure began to tell. It wasn't obvious to Bob, who kept plugging ahead. But those around him could see the damage that was being done.

"Finally, a wise, honest person to whom I was accountable said to me, 'You aren't going to make it another year. And I want you to make it fifty more years. You can't burn the candle at both ends. If you're going to be true to God, you have to find a Sabbath.'"

It was a tough message to hear, but one Bob took to heart. "I wanted to fix everybody; I *still* want to fix everybody. But you *can't* fix everybody."

Think of your life as a candle. Briefly describe it, and take careful note of whether it's burning brightly or dimly and why. Then describe whether it's burning at one end or two—and why.

If you're in youth ministry for the long haul, where's your Sabbath? your daily time to be refreshed in your relationship with God and his people?

46. MUD BOWL
Ken Davis

W hile Ken Davis was serving a church in Minnesota, he organized a youth group "mud bowl."

The idea of a mud bowl is to peel back the sod in a field, flood the area, create a mud swamp fit for a pig, and then get disgustingly dirty playing games in it.

"Actually, I got in trouble for two reasons," remembers Ken. "First, there were the kids who had to go to the hospital in an ambulance." Apparently there were jagged rocks in part of the mud bowl that Ken hadn't found. Several kids *did* find them.

The second reason was the filth the kids tracked into the church building.

"We tried so hard to keep the church clean," says Ken. "Kids took off their shoes, and we toweled kids off. But they still dripped water on pews donated by people who'd been dead about nine hundred years."

After the event, Ken was chastised by both the church and his youth ministry board of directors.

"The kids didn't destroy a thing, but we made extra work for a few people," says Ken, "and that *mattered*."

Ken didn't think much more about his mud bowl experience until a few years later when he spoke at a church in Ohio.

"It was a brand, spanking new building," says Ken, who was surprised to discover a mud bowl for three hundred kids in progress. "A fire truck sprayed water on some of the excavation dirt," he remembers. "It was a perfect site."

What amazed Ken was the presence of ten old guys who had already spread black plastic over the entire sanctuary: on the pews, the floors, *everything*. As kids lined up to enter the building, the men took turns spraying the kids with the fire hose and then giving each teenager a towel.

Ken was choked up at their obvious dedication to servanthood and youth ministry. "I could hardly speak, I was so touched," he says.

Ken asked an elderly man holding the fire hose why he'd given the time to help. "I was expecting an 'I just love to see kids come to the Lord' response," says Ken. "But he turned and looked at me and said, 'I don't know about the rest of the guys, but I do it for *this.*'"

"Live as free men, but do not use your freedom as a cover-up for evil; live as servants of God. Show proper respect to everyone: Love the brotherhood of believers, fear God, honor the king"

1 Peter 2:16-17.

"He winked and turned the hose on a guy. He blasted the guy about thirty feet as he hosed him off."

Ken can't help comparing how the leaders of the two "mud bowl churches" felt about using their buildings. "I learned that buildings are made for people," he says. "Buildings should serve people, not the other way around."

Ken cautions youth workers to think through the impact any activity might have on a facility and take appropriate precautions. He suggests doing this, not just because you might get in trouble, but out of love for people who believe their church building should be a place of dignity and quiet.

How well do you protect your congregation's building? Are you intentional about preventing problems? communicating what you want to do before you try it? How would your church janitor and pastor answer those questions?

47. 365-24-7
Walt Mueller

When Walt Mueller first jumped into youth ministry, he dove straight into the deep end of the pool.

"I worked with college students, high school students, and middle school kids," he remembers. "I did about forty hours a week with the college students, then forty more with each of the other groups. I wasn't married, I was crazy, and I was just loving it."

"All my waking hours were spent on ministry," he recalls, but not with pride.

"If you're looking for an example of setting bad habits, there's one right there," Walt confesses. He found it hard to pull back from that pace over the years.

"I'm at a point where I'm managing that tendency; it's not an issue anymore. But initially I set some bad patterns," he says.

Walt says that, when he married Lisa and their children began arriving, "it became obvious that I was spending too much time in ministry with others and not enough with my own family."

"Once you have a spouse and then kids, if you aren't feeling a tug between being home with your family and out with the youth group, something's wrong. If you still just want to be with the youth group, you need to take stock of your priorities because you're going to leave your spouse and your kids in the dust.

"You reach a point where you start to say, 'On Friday and Saturday night, I want to be home with my own kids.' It's not that you don't want to do youth ministry anymore, it's that you want to spend more time with your own family. If you don't, your wife (or husband) will see your ministry as your mistress—and that's the *last* thing you want."

How many hours a week do you work? If it's more than fifty, ask yourself why. Is there anyone else paying for your dedication to youth ministry? Who? How do they feel about it?

48. FILL 'ER UP
Dan Slatter

While in Chichester, England, Dan Slatter worked with teenagers in a housing project. The poverty-stricken kids seldom got out of the housing project, especially to attend fun events.

"Some of these kids' lives were completely screwed up," says Dan. They lived in "extreme situations, and none of them were Christians."

Dan and a volunteer decided to take the kids ice skating. "We said, 'Let's take them out, have some fun, and get to know them,'" he remembers. "We put sixteen of them in the back of a minibus. And they were head cases [American translation: berserk kids], all of them."

Dan made it to the skating rink with the kids. On the way home, they stopped to buy gas. "My friend, who was driving the minibus, realized as he was pulling out that he'd put petrol in a diesel engine."

The van expressed its gratitude by quickly puttering to a stop.

"We were stuck twenty miles from home on the side of the road," says Dan, "with these kids going *mad*. Sixteen head cases we're trying to control while we waited for roadside service. It seemed like we were there *forever*."

Dumb mistakes, oversights, missed details...

If you haven't pulled one yet, you will. Odds are good that it'll happen in full view of your kids.

How you handle an embarrassing gaffe will do more for—or to—your ministry than most Bible lessons you deliver. It authenticates your faith for your kids and gives them permission to admit their mistakes when they pull a bonehead move.

How do you respond when your kids see you do something stupid? Why?

BONUS! BLUE, BLACK, RED, AND WHITE
Les Christie

Les Christie had just arrived as the part-time youth worker in a Garden Grove, California, church. Noticing that the youth room was painted a dingy, hospital-white color, Les suggested to the kids that they paint the room.

Les rounded up cans of donated paint and met his kids at 5:00 a.m. the next Saturday. When kids couldn't agree what color to paint the room, they decided on a compromise. They would paint each of the four walls a *different* color.

After painting one wall white, another black, and the last two blue and red, Les and his crew cleaned up and went out for breakfast. Mission accomplished.

What Les didn't know was that another group met in the room while the youth group was at the first worship service. The senior citizens used the same room.

During the first worship service, Les sat on the stage, beaming. He felt proud of the work his group had accomplished—until the senior pastor slid into the chair next to him and told him the senior citizens were *really* upset.

> *"Everyone must submit himself to the governing authorities, for there is no authority except that which God has established. The authorities that exist have been established by God. Consequently, he who rebels against the authority is rebelling against what God has instituted, and those who do so will bring judgment on themselves"*
>
> Romans 13:1-2.

"He said, 'You can kiss your job good-bye. I can't save you. You're dead meat.'"

So Les marched into the senior citizens' class. It was a bold move, given the circumstances.

"I entered the room and, before they could say anything, I asked if they'd noticed the room had been painted. They had. I then told them how excited I was to work in a church where the high schoolers were so spiritual.

"I explained that the wall on the left was blue to symbolize heaven. The wall on the right was red to stand for the blood of Christ. The wall behind them was black, which stood for sin, and they were facing away from that wall. The wall at the front of the room was white, which stood for purity.

"I then grabbed the kids and told them, 'Look, if anyone asks you why we picked those colors, here's what you should say.'"

While Les would never advocate that a youth worker lie to a room full of seniors, he's amazed at the impact of his desperate story. "The church kept those colors in that room for the next *fourteen years,* because nobody would paint over the blood of Christ."

Youth workers are an impulsive group. You *have* to be to take advantage of opportunities and keep up with the kids. But being impulsive isn't always a virtue.

"I should have asked permission. I should have checked it out with someone over me, but I was impulsive," says Les.

If "It's better to ask forgiveness than get permission" is a motto of your youth ministry, why? What does that motto say about you? What sort of standard are you holding up for your kids?

49. THE DISAPPEARING STUDENTS
Larry Lindquist

During his first youth ministry, Larry Lindquist orchestrated a bike trip across Wisconsin to a national youth event.

"A portion of the students were in the biking group. The rest were coming by van," remembers Larry. A van loaded with camping equipment followed the bikers.

Because there were several levels of biking ability, Larry's group stretched out along the daily trail…too *far* along the daily trail.

A girl in the group who had fallen far behind stopped at a small restaurant to rest. Not seeing her, the follow-up van passed her by. Then, as she shared her story of fatigue, a guy offered to throw her bike in the back of his pickup and drive her to that evening's campsite.

Larry was helping his group set up camp that night when he noticed the girl was missing. "No one had a clue," he says. "I sent scouts back the way we came. They found nothing. We called the police and learned nothing. We prayed. Then a pickup drove into our camp. Out jumped our missing girl, who was all smiles until she saw our faces."

The missing biker explained that the guy who gave her a lift had showed her the town, introduced his family, and given her quite the tour.

"God was too good to me that day," says Larry. "The guy who drove her really *was* a nice guy."

Larry learned a valuable lesson. Never assume teenagers will make good decisions. "As much as you think students understand, you *must* explain clearly what are and are not acceptable departures from your plan."

Assumptions are killers, yet we all make them.

What are you assuming your kids understand or will do?

50. OOPS
Andy Hansen

At his youth group's winter retreat, Andy Hansen decided to play a prank on the girls in one of the girls' cabins. He waited until after dark, filled a bucket with cold water, and sprinted across the frozen ground to a cabin full of young ladies who were already tucked in for the night.

"I kicked the door open and threw the water," says Andy. "I thought it was the girls' cabin and there were girls in there. Unfortunately, I threw the water on the three *adult* women sponsors.

"They all smacked their heads on the bunks above them as they looked up at me standing there, giggling—until I saw their faces.

"*That* one didn't go over real well," remembers Andy.

Good clean fun is something you need in youth ministry but never at the expense of someone else. The soaked volunteers forgave Andy—eventually—and the retreat went on. Activities that embarrass a kid or leave someone feeling stupid have no place in a ministry built on trust and acceptance.

How safe do teenagers feel participating in your group's activities? How well do you communicate your respect and esteem?

ALL-STAR BIOS

Larry Acosta is president of Hispanic Ministry Center and KIDWORKS. When he was about ten, Larry went to a county fair with friends who each stole grab bags from a booth. "I went last because I knew it was wrong, and I'm the one who got caught," says Larry, who says that experience scared him. Find Larry online at www.hmconline .org (pp. 25, 92).

Jeff Baxter is a speaker for Kingdom Building Ministries, and is a youth worker in Greenwood, Indiana. Entering high school, Jeff was a strapping 4 feet, 10 inches. While that doesn't qualify as a mistake, it apparently felt like one (p. 59).

Bryan Belknap, a former campus minister, is the Mind Over Media editor at youthministry.com. His biggest mistake as a child? "Having my hair feathered and long—in junior high." Say no more. Bryan also wrote *Group's BlockBuster Movie Illustrations* (p. 67).

Anthony "Tony" Campolo is an author, speaker, and founder of the Evangelical Association for the Promotion of Education. We caught up with him long enough to find out about a youth ministry gaffe; we didn't push it for a story about something he did as a child (p. 16).

Les Christie is chair of the youth ministry department at San Jose Christian College and a prolific author. He's been in youth ministry for thirty-four years. Les and his younger sister are now best friends, but, when they were children, Les convinced his sister she could float off the garage roof by holding umbrellas (pp. 11, 20, 52, 77, 101).

Lyman Coleman has been painting outside the lines in youth ministry for forty years as a youth leader, trainer, teller of stories, dreamer of dreams, and teller of truth. Yet this man who found ways to connect the youth culture with the church was straight-laced as a child. "I sort of wish I'd acted up more when I was young so I wouldn't have had to get it out of my system in my twenties," he says (p. 64).

John Cutshall is an author, former Bible college dean, and long-term youth worker who's currently serving a church in Illinois. He remembers that, while receiving a spanking as a child, the yardstick his mother was using broke. "And I *laughed*," he says regretfully (pp. 44, 62, 95).

Ken Davis is president of Dynamic Communications International, a best-selling author, featured speaker for Promise Keepers, and a frequent Focus on the Family guest. While in a high school English class studying Shakespeare's *Macbeth*, Ken and his classmates came upon the line, "Out, damned spot! Out, I say!" "I raised my hand and suggested several other adjectives that could be dropped in there," he remembers. "I got in a *lot* of trouble over that" (p. 98).

Karen Dockrey has worked with youth for close to thirty years and written nearly as many books. One of the best things about Karen is that she's still stretching, growing, and making mistakes. Karen is the author of *Jr. High Retreats and Lock-Ins* (Group Publishing, 1990) (p. 40).

Dan Gilliam has brought music and art to youth groups and congregations for the past dozen years. As a child he broke his nose—twice—because he kept walking up a slippery set of steps with his hands in his pockets. "I was a slow learner," says Dan. Contact Dan at www.DanGilliam.com (pp. 58, 71).

Andy Hansen has been in youth ministry for nearly thirty years and is currently director of conferences for Christ in Youth. Andy presents youth ministry workshops around America and overseas. When Andy was young, his mother warned him to not touch a glowing object on the kitchen table. Andy ignored her. "It was a waffle iron, and it was *hot*," says Andy, who ended up at the emergency room with third-degree burns (pp. 42, 87, 104).

Doug Herman has served as a youth worker since 1981 and spoken to more than a million teenagers about abstinence and love. When he was young, Doug's father built a go-cart for him. During the initial run, Doug realized the cart wouldn't stop. "I did finally stop it," says Doug, "but I stopped it with a tree" (p. 48).

Monty Hipp, a national youth speaker and all-around communicator, is the executive vice president of First Priority. When he was fifteen, Monty dated two girls who were friends. At the same time. "I learned some very brutal lessons there." Contact Monty at www.firstpriority.org (pp. 35, 81).

Dan Jessup is currently area director of Young Life in Colorado Springs and an adjunct youth ministry professor for Fuller Theological Seminary. As a youngster, Dan slipped off into a field behind his house to smoke a cigarette, not realizing he was in full view of the kitchen window…and his mother (pp. 19, 80).

Jim Kochenburger has developed and written books, videos, and curriculum for several publishers and is currently employed at Group Publishing, Inc. When Jim was seven, he found some questionable pictures and took them to a friend's house. "I held them up to his window, but didn't notice his mother was standing right behind him." Check out Jim's new book, *The Top 20 Messages for Youth Ministry* (Group Publishing, 2001), as well as *Shake & Bake Messages for Youth Ministry* (Group Publishing, 2000) (pp. 23, 32).

Scott Larson is co-founder of Straight Ahead Ministries, a national organization focused on ministering to juvenile offenders. He didn't recall any specific mistakes he made as a child; we suspect a cover-up and are investigating. Scott has authored both *At Risk: Bringing Hope to Hurting Teenagers* (Group Publishing, 1999) and *Risk in Our Midst* (Group Publishing, 2000) (p. 22).

Bob Laurent has been a keynote speaker at more than twelve hundred national conferences and is dean of the graduate school at Bethel College. As a young child, he believed he wasn't any good unless he performed well. "I was becoming a human 'doing' rather than a human 'being,' " he says. "What a revelation to me when I realized God could love me no matter what" (pp. 84, 97).

Rick Lawrence is a youth trend-watcher, speaker, and executive editor of GROUP Magazine. "When I was ten years old or so, my dream was to be an NFL quarterback," says Rick, "and I took every opportunity I could to throw something—anything—at moving targets." One winter day, Rick played quarterback…with a rock…and his little sister. Despite her efforts to dodge the rock, Rick's perfect aim hit its mark. "For three seconds I was thrilled at my feat, then she turned around and I could see blood seeping through her windbreaker hood," he recalls. Needless to say, Rick was in big trouble (and was sidelined for the rest of the season). Rick is the author of *Trendwatch* (Group Publishing, 2000) (p. 23).

Larry Lindquist is assistant professor of youth and family ministries and educational ministry at Denver Seminary. He has served in several churches as associate pastor of education and music. While a teenager, Larry was drag racing and was spotted by a cop. "The lights went on and I pulled into an alley, then into some guy's garage where I cut off my headlights, scrunched down in the seat, and prayed." No, he wasn't found out…until now. Call your local police department at once (pp. 14, 60, 103).

Ron Luce is the founder of Teen Mania Ministries and Acquire The Fire. Before becoming a Christian, Ron once cut classes to sneak off and drink beer. He managed to catch the school bus back home and, on the trip, realized the beer was coming back up—fast. "I aimed for the window, but I didn't make it" (p. 39).

Rolland Martinson has been in youth ministry in one capacity or another for forty years. He's been a youth director, associate pastor, senior pastor, national youth coordinator, and seminary professor (p. 72).

Randy Matthews can be counted among Christian rock's founding fathers—and for twenty-five years he's had a tremendous impact on both audiences and a generation of musicians. It wasn't without personal cost, though. "My mother was right about turning the music down a little bit," confesses Randy, "Because I've lost the edge on my ears after thirty years of rock and roll" (p. 45).

Walt Mueller is the president of the Center for Parent/Youth Understanding, a nonprofit organization that helps churches, schools, and community organizations in their efforts to strengthen families. He's been involved in youth and family ministry for more than twenty-one years. When Walt was in eighth grade, he skipped youth group one night to hang out with a friend, thinking his father would never find out. His father was the pastor (pp. 30, 99).

Steve Munds once shot his little brother in the foot with a BB gun, a shot that required toe surgery. "I didn't *mean* to shoot him," claims Steve, "I was just trying to scare him." It worked. When not abusing siblings, Steve is a speaker, a youth pastor at Living Word Christian Center, and a musician. His most recent CDs are *No One Like You* and *C'mon and Dance* (pp. 19, 51, 81).

Mike Nappa is a best-selling author, president of Nappaland Communications, and a former youth pastor. When he was in seventh grade, he gave a "wedgie" to a guy who was twice his size. "I had a knot on the back of my head for about two weeks," he says. Mike co-authored *Get Real: Making Core Christian Beliefs Relevant to Teenagers* (Group Publishing, 1997) (pp. 31, 88).

G. Keith Olson, Ph.D., established Family Consultation Service, a psychotherapy service center, in 1971. He wrote *Counseling Teenagers* (Group Publishing, 1984) (pp. 63, 95).

Les Parrott III, Ph.D., is an author, speaker, and professor of psychology and co-director of the Center for Relationship Development at Seattle Pacific University. Les and his wife, Dr. Leslie Parrott, were recently chosen to be scholars-in-residence for Oklahoma's first-ever statewide marriage initiative. When he was seven, Les jumped on his parents' bed frame and broke it. "I thought that was the end of my life," says Les, who tried to repair the damage by placing encyclopedias under one corner of the bed. "Half the bookshelf was missing; that's how they discovered the problem" (pp. 57, 66).

Darrell Pearson is assistant professor of youth ministry at Eastern College. He's also known by junior high leaders as a presenter for Wild Truth. While in elementary school, Darrell let two other guys convince him that they could skip recess, leave the school property, and go buy candy at a nearby store. One of the guys was an informer who went straight to the principal. Says Darrell, "I learned I needed to pick my friends better" (pp. 34, 55, 90).

Duffy Robbins is chair of the department of youth ministry at Eastern College in Pennsylvania and a twenty-five year veteran of youth ministry (p. 49).

Dwight Robertson is founder and president of Kingdom Building Ministries. His ultimate ministry goal is to see a vast worldwide army of new Kingdom laborers raised up and trained as disciples (p. 76).

Barry St. Clair has trained thousands of new youth workers through Reach Out Ministries. As a child, Barry *hated* choir, but his mother made him go. So Barry and his buddy, Charles, entertained themselves by stabbing each other with pencils. Charles won when he placed a sharpened pencil in the cushions where Barry would land squarely on it. Barry reports there's still a mark, but we didn't have the nerve to ask for visual confirmation (pp. 47, 92).

Joani Schultz is chief creative officer of Group Publishing, Inc., and has over twenty years of youth ministry experience. As a young child, Joani occasionally got so angry with her parents that she ran away from home. Fortunately, living in the country, she could only make it to the next house—which was where her uncle lived. Joani and Thom Schultz have authored *Why Nobody Learns Much of Anything at Church: And How to Fix It* (Group Publishing, 1993), *The Dirt on Learning* (Group Publishing, 1999), and *Do It! Active Learning in Youth Ministry* (Group Publishing, 2000) (pp. 19, 21, 64, 91).

Thom Schultz is founder and CEO of Group Publishing, Inc., and a former youth worker. While in high school, Thom and his buddies drove Thom's old jeep through open fields at night, hunting rabbits. The goal was to stay with the rabbit as it bolted around a pitch-black field until the rabbit tired and stopped. They'd then

leap from the jeep, pet it, and release it. Imagine Thom's surprise when one night a rabbit bolted into tall grass that was hiding a ditch. A deep ditch. A deep ditch that swallowed the front end of the jeep (pp. 26, 78).

Dan Slatter oversees Warehouse, a youth church in England that includes students between the ages of twelve and twenty-two. When he was fifteen, he and some friends "bunked off school" to go hang out in an empty building. It was cold, so they started a fire in a fireplace and then decided to set fire to the entire house. "I was a bit of a naughty boy when I was young" (pp. 68, 100).

Tim Smith is an author, conference speaker, consultant with Heritage Builders, and pastor of family life and parenting at Calvary Community Church. While in middle school, Tim saw a big kid picking on a little kid and interceded by asking, "Why don't you pick on someone your own size?" The bully agreed, and proceeded to beat up Tim. "I got in one hit," Tim remembers, "*just* as the principal walked into sight." Check out Tim's book *Nurturing the Soul of the Youth Worker* (Group Publishing, 1999) (pp. 12, 69).

Dave Stone has been in and around youth ministry for nearly forty years, and says, "I'll always be a youth minister. You grow *into* youth ministry, not *out* of it." When he was ten, Dave and a friend decided to sell hub caps to raise money. Within a few hours they'd found 104, most of which, unfortunately, came off used cars parked on the car lot where his father worked (pp. 15, 31, 53).

Lynn Ziegenfuss is Youth for Christ's senior vice president of people development and oversees recruitment and training. When she was eight years old, she accidentally broke a family heirloom: an antique glass decanter. Lynn's mother was unhappy but used the experience to let Lynn know she was worth more than any heirloom (p. 74).